ULTIMATE SMOOTHIE SENSATIONS

200 Quick & Healthy Recipes for Vibrant Living

Evelyn Freshwell

Copyright © 2023 Evelyn Freshwell

All rights reserved.

ULTIMATE SMOOTHIE SENSATIONS

CONTENTS

Introduction	8
Disclaimer and Legal Notice	10
The Health Benefits of Smoothies	12
How to Make a Smoothie	14
Secrets to Making the Best Smoothie Ever	15
Tips for Health-Conscious Readers	16
Recipe 1: Berry Blast Smoothie	18
Recipe 2: Green Goddess Smoothie	18
Recipe 3: Tropical Paradise Smoothie	18
Recipe 4: Peanut Butter Power Smoothie	19
Recipe 5: Citrus Sunshine Smoothie	19
Recipe 6: Chocolate Banana Bliss Smoothie	19
Recipe 7: Almond Joy Smoothie	20
Recipe 8: Pomegranate Berry Burst Smoothie	20
Recipe 9: Spinach Mango Delight Smoothie	20
Recipe 10: Avocado Mint Marvel Smoothie	21
Recipe 11: Cherry Almond Bliss Smoothie	21
Recipe 12: Minty Pineapple Kale Smoothie	21
Recipe 13: Raspberry Lemonade Smoothie	22
Recipe 14: Oatmeal Cookie Smoothie	22
Recipe 15: Carrot Cake Smoothie	23
Recipe 16: Mango Basil Delight Smoothie	23
Recipe 17: Blueberry Bliss Smoothie	23
Recipe 18: Peachy Keen Smoothie	24
Recipe 19: Cranberry Orange Zest Smoothie	24
Recipe 20: Coconut Raspberry Dream Smoothie	25
Recipe 21: Matcha Green Tea Smoothie	25
Recipe 22: Strawberry Shortcake Smoothie	25
Recipe 23: Spicy Mango Tango Smoothie	26
Recipe 24: Banana Bread Smoothie	26
Recipe 25: Choco-Nut Heaven Smoothie	26
Recipe 26: Vanilla Berry Swirl Smoothie	27
Recipe 27: Golden Turmeric Elixir Smoothie	27
Recipe 28: Raspberry Chocolate Indulgence Smoothie	28
Recipe 29: Pina Colada Paradise Smoothie	28
Recipe 30: Detox Green Smoothie	28
Recipe 31: Mint Chocolate Chip Smoothie	29
Recipe 32: Sweet Potato Pie Smoothie	29
Recipe 33: Cucumber Melon Cooler Smoothie	29
Recipe 34: Pistachio Paradise Smoothie	30
Recipe 35: Mango Ginger Zinger Smoothie	30
Recipe 36: Raspberry Avocado Refresher Smoothie	31
Recipe 37: Cherry Chocolate Delight Smoothie	31

ULTIMATE SMOOTHIE SENSATIONS

Recipe 38: Pomegranate Green Tea Boost Smoothie — 31
Recipe 39: Blackberry Basil Bliss Smoothie — 32
Recipe 40: Carrot Cake Detox Smoothie — 32
Recipe 41: Mango Turmeric Tango Smoothie — 32
Recipe 42: Cherry Almond Spinach Smoothie — 33
Recipe 43: Papaya Passion Smoothie — 33
Recipe 44: Berry Basil Blast Smoothie — 34
Recipe 45: Cantaloupe Cooler Smoothie — 34
Recipe 46: Peach Basil Breeze Smoothie — 34
Recipe 47: Blueberry Lavender Dream Smoothie — 35
Recipe 48: Raspberry Rose Elixir Smoothie — 35
Recipe 49: Ginger Pear Spice Smoothie — 35
Recipe 50: Coconut Berry Bliss Smoothie — 36
Recipe 51: Pineapple Ginger Zing Smoothie — 36
Recipe 52: Vanilla Fig Delight Smoothie — 37
Recipe 53: Minty Watermelon Refresher Smoothie — 37
Recipe 54: Cacao Berry Protein Boost Smoothie — 37
Recipe 55: Chia Cherry Chiller Smoothie — 38
Recipe 56: Spirulina Blueberry Blast Smoothie — 38
Recipe 57: Raspberry Lemon Verbena Smoothie — 38
Recipe 58: Turmeric Mango Sunrise Smoothie — 39
Recipe 59: Blackberry Sage Infusion Smoothie — 39
Recipe 60: Coconut Kiwi Kale Kick Smoothie — 40
Recipe 61: Mango Matcha Madness Smoothie — 40
Recipe 62: Chocolate Raspberry Love Smoothie — 40
Recipe 63: Peachy Green Goddess Smoothie — 41
Recipe 64: Blueberry Lavender Lemonade Smoothie — 41
Recipe 65: Banana Nut Bread Smoothie — 41
Recipe 66: Cucumber Mint Cooler Smoothie — 42
Recipe 67: Mocha Almond Dream Smoothie — 42
Recipe 68: Mango Pineapple Paradise Smoothie — 43
Recipe 69: Raspberry Coconut Crush Smoothie — 43
Recipe 70: Green Tea Mango Zen Smoothie — 43
Recipe 71: Papaya Passionflower Bliss Smoothie — 44
Recipe 72: Apricot Almond Sunrise Smoothie — 44
Recipe 73: Strawberry Basil Infusion Smoothie — 45
Recipe 74: Minty Pineapple Cooler Smoothie — 45
Recipe 75: Raspberry Hibiscus Harmony Smoothie — 45
Recipe 76: Goji Berry Citrus Boost Smoothie — 46
Recipe 77: Cherry Vanilla Serenity Smoothie — 46
Recipe 78: Ginger Pear Immunity Boost Smoothie — 46
Recipe 79: Figgy Blueberry Bliss Smoothie — 47
Recipe 80: Banana Cocoa Crunch Smoothie — 47
Recipe 81: Avocado Mint Chocolate Chip Smoothie — 48

Recipe 82: Raspberry Mango Basil Bliss Smoothie --- 48
Recipe 83: Spinach Pineapple Paradise Smoothie -- 48
Recipe 84: Blueberry Coconut Chia Smoothie -- 49
Recipe 85: Peach Raspberry Rose Smoothie -- 49
Recipe 86: Cucumber Kiwi Kale Crush Smoothie --- 50
Recipe 87: Mango Pine Nut Euphoria Smoothie--- 50
Recipe 88: Orange Carrot Turmeric Twist Smoothie--- 50
Recipe 89: Mixed Berry Maca Magic Smoothie -- 51
Recipe 90: Coconut Mango Macadamia Smoothie-- 51
Recipe 91: Pomegranate Berry Burst Smoothie -- 52
Recipe 92: Turmeric Pineapple Glow Smoothie--- 52
Recipe 93: Dragon Fruit Berry Bliss Smoothie --- 52
Recipe 94: Mango Turmeric Sunrise Smoothie-- 53
Recipe 95: Acai Berry Powerhouse Smoothie --- 53
Recipe 96: Matcha Green Tea Elixir Smoothie-- 54
Recipe 97: Coconut Mango Spirulina Splash Smoothie -------------------------------------- 54
Recipe 98: Cacao Peanut Butter Protein Punch Smoothie ---------------------------------- 54
Recipe 99: Cherry Almond Chia Delight Smoothie --- 55
Recipe 100: Golden Turmeric Coconut Smoothie --- 55
Recipe 101: Mango Turmeric Lassi Smoothie -- 56
Recipe 102: Berry Citrus Beet Boost Smoothie --- 56
Recipe 103: Green Goddess Avocado Spinach Smoothie ------------------------------------ 56
Recipe 104: Peach Basil Breeze Smoothie -- 57
Recipe 105: Coconut Blue Majik Dream Smoothie-- 57
Recipe 106: Tropical Carrot Pineapple Punch Smoothie------------------------------------ 58
Recipe 107: Raspberry Rosemary Refresher Smoothie ------------------------------------- 58
Recipe 108: Orange Carrot Ginger Zest Smoothie --- 58
Recipe 109: Cacao Raspberry Protein Bliss Smoothie -------------------------------------- 59
Recipe 110: Chia Cherry Chocolate Delight Smoothie-------------------------------------- 59
Recipe 111: Minty Melon Cooler Smoothie --- 60
Recipe 112: Cranberry Apple Cinnamon Smoothie -- 60
Recipe 113: Papaya Coconut Lime Smoothie -- 60
Recipe 114: Fig Pistachio Delight Smoothie --- 61
Recipe 115: Blackberry Lavender Lemonade Smoothie ------------------------------------ 61
Recipe 116: Apricot Cardamom Cream Smoothie -- 62
Recipe 117: Cucumber Pineapple Mint Refresher Smoothie ------------------------------ 62
Recipe 118: Raspberry Mango Tango Smoothie--- 62
Recipe 119: Matcha Berry Bliss Smoothie-- 63
Recipe 120: Chocolate Cherry Almond Indulgence Smoothie ---------------------------- 63
Recipe 121: Spiced Apple Pie Smoothie -- 64
Recipe 122: Coconut Kiwi Kale Kick Smoothie --- 64
Recipe 123: Gingered Pear Smoothie-- 64
Recipe 124: Mango Basil Bliss Smoothie-- 65
Recipe 125: Vanilla Date Delight Smoothie --- 65

ULTIMATE SMOOTHIE SENSATIONS

Recipe 126: Raspberry Coconut Chia Crush Smoothie --- 66
Recipe 127: Peach Ginger Turmeric Twist Smoothie --- 66
Recipe 128: Blueberry Basil Blast Smoothie --- 66
Recipe 129: Cacao Hazelnut Heaven Smoothie --- 67
Recipe 130: Mint Chocolate Chip Avocado Smoothie --- 67
Recipe 131: Pineapple Turmeric Zinger Smoothie --- 68
Recipe 132: Strawberry Basil Serenity Smoothie --- 68
Recipe 133: Coconut Papaya Paradise Smoothie --- 68
Recipe 134: Banana Nutmeg Euphoria Smoothie --- 69
Recipe 135: Raspberry Pineapple Mint Magic Smoothie --- 69
Recipe 136: Cucumber Spinach Kiwi Cleanse Smoothie --- 69
Recipe 137: Blueberry Lavender Love Smoothie --- 70
Recipe 138: Fig Vanilla Dream Smoothie --- 70
Recipe 139: Mango Coconut Cardamom Smoothie --- 71
Recipe 140: Cherry Vanilla Almond Bliss Smoothie --- 71
Recipe 141: Melon Mint Medley Smoothie --- 71
Recipe 142: Cinnamon Pear Pleasure Smoothie --- 72
Recipe 143: Kiwi Lime Kale Kick Smoothie --- 72
Recipe 144: Banana Berry Basil Bliss Smoothie --- 72
Recipe 145: Raspberry Rose Refresher Smoothie --- 73
Recipe 146: Minty Chocolate Chip Delight Smoothie --- 73
Recipe 147: Chia Berry Citrus Splash Smoothie --- 74
Recipe 148: Peach Raspberry Rosemary Smoothie --- 74
Recipe 149: Orange Carrot Turmeric Twist Smoothie --- 74
Recipe 150: Mango Pineapple Basil Bliss Smoothie --- 75
Recipe 151: Cocoa Banana Peanut Butter Crunch Smoothie --- 75
Recipe 152: Blackberry Sage Sensation Smoothie --- 76
Recipe 153: Pineapple Coconut Matcha Madness Smoothie --- 76
Recipe 154: Fig Date Walnut Wonder Smoothie --- 76
Recipe 155: Mango Spinach Ginger Glow Smoothie --- 77
Recipe 156: Blueberry Basil Blast Smoothie --- 77
Recipe 157: Cherry Almond Spice Smoothie --- 78
Recipe 158: Papaya Pineapple Basil Bliss Smoothie --- 78
Recipe 159: Strawberry Mango Maca Marvel Smoothie --- 78
Recipe 160: Coconut Cherry Chia Delight Smoothie --- 79
Recipe 161: Pomegranate Blueberry Basil Boost Smoothie --- 79
Recipe 162: Cucumber Mint Green Goodness Smoothie --- 79
Recipe 163: Raspberry Mango Macadamia Magic Smoothie --- 80
Recipe 164: Carrot Pineapple Turmeric Twist Smoothie --- 80
Recipe 165: Avocado Kale Citrus Splash Smoothie --- 81
Recipe 166: Spinach Mango Ginger Zing Smoothie --- 81
Recipe 167: Strawberry Pineapple Basil Bliss Smoothie --- 81
Recipe 168: Cocoa Coconut Almond Indulgence Smoothie --- 82
Recipe 169: Peach Raspberry Rosemary Refresh Smoothie --- 82

ULTIMATE SMOOTHIE SENSATIONS

Recipe 170: Mango Pineapple Basil Bliss Smoothie — 83
Recipe 171: Raspberry Lemonade Twist Smoothie — 83
Recipe 172: Banana Chia Seed Power Smoothie — 83
Recipe 173: Blueberry Lavender Lemonade Smoothie — 84
Recipe 174: Orange Mango Carrot Sunshine Smoothie — 84
Recipe 175: Cocoa Banana Berry Bliss Smoothie — 84
Recipe 176: Pineapple Kale Coconut Cooler Smoothie — 85
Recipe 177: Mango Turmeric Ginger Gold Smoothie — 85
Recipe 178: Berry Spinach Flax Fuel Smoothie — 86
Recipe 179: Coconut Kiwi Lime Paradise Smoothie — 86
Recipe 180: Cherry Vanilla Protein Punch Smoothie — 86
Recipe 181: Raspberry Mango Basil Bliss Smoothie — 87
Recipe 182: Papaya Pineapple Mint Medley Smoothie — 87
Recipe 183: Blueberry Almond Butter Crunch Smoothie — 87
Recipe 184: Chia Coconut Berry Burst Smoothie — 88
Recipe 185: Mango Turmeric Citrus Zing Smoothie — 88
Recipe 186: Peach Raspberry Rosewater Elegance Smoothie — 88
Recipe 187: Cocoa Banana Coconut Crunch Smoothie — 89
Recipe 188: Kiwi Spinach Green Goddess Smoothie — 89
Recipe 189: Strawberry Pine Nut Dream Smoothie — 90
Recipe 190: Orange Carrot Ginger Energizer Smoothie — 90
Recipe 191: Minty Melon Cucumber Cooler Smoothie — 90
Recipe 192: Cinnamon Apple Oatmeal Smoothie — 91
Recipe 193: Cherry Coconut Lime Delight Smoothie — 91
Recipe 194: Peach Raspberry Pecan Pleasure Smoothie — 91
Recipe 195: Avocado Blueberry Basil Beauty Smoothie — 92
Recipe 196: Mango Pine Nut Paradise Smoothie — 92
Recipe 197: Strawberry Almond Poppy Seed Smoothie — 92
Recipe 198: Pineapple Chia Coconut Bliss Smoothie — 93
Recipe 199: Cocoa Raspberry Hazelnut Heaven Smoothie — 93
Recipe 200: Orange Carrot Turmeric Radiance Smoothie — 94
Conclusion: Sip Your Way to Vibrant Living — 96

ULTIMATE SMOOTHIE SENSATIONS

Introduction

In the midst of all the activity of modern life, it's easy to lose sight of what's most important—your physical and mental well-being—in favor of meeting ever-increasing demands. Despite our best intentions, it can be difficult to make healthy decisions in the face of everyday stress and pressure.

Here comes "Ultimate Smoothie Sensations: 200 Quick and Healthy Recipes for Vibrant Living," a carefully produced manual for anyone who wants to go on a life-changing path toward better health and vitality via the power of smoothies. This book is a beacon of light for anybody who has ever felt hopeless in the face of fad diets, contradictory health advice, or the simple difficulty of combining healthy options into a hectic lifestyle.

You may be wondering, "Why do I need this book?"

What follows are not just recipes but a philosophy, one that promotes the view that health is not a sacrifice but a cause for joy. This book will change your life by showing you how to harness the extraordinary power of entire, nutrient-dense foods in the form of tasty, simple smoothies. These aren't only recipes; they're invitations to reawaken and rediscover a way of life in which nutritious food can also be delicious.

In these sections, you'll learn about the incredible chemistry between components meant to strengthen your body and mind, as well as your taste sensations. Each dish is a celebration of the philosophy that health and happiness do not need sacrifice but, rather, the most extraordinary, life-altering forms of pleasure. This book is essential because it explains all you need to know about superfoods, antioxidants, and the pleasure of eating food that loves you back.

Have you had enough of feeling lethargic and dreaming of a more energized and fit self? There is an answer in this book. It is your passage to a world where health isn't a pipe dream but an attainable goal. These dishes will become your trusted friends on the way to a healthy lifestyle, whether you're just starting out or a seasoned health fanatic.

Get ready for a journey in which every smoothie you make is a step toward vitality and every dish you try is an act of self-love. This book is more than a compilation of recipes; it is your ally in exploring the amazing, baffling, and potent terrain of thriving life. Get out your mixer, and we'll start mixing. Your exciting new life has just begun.

Disclaimer and Legal Notice

The information, recipes, and suggestions presented in this book, "Ultimate Smoothie Sensations: 200 Quick & Healthy Recipes for Vibrant Living," are intended for entertainment and informational purposes only. The author and the publisher take no responsibility for the results obtained or not obtained from using the information provided in this book, despite the fact that they have taken all reasonable measures to assure the accuracy and completeness of the content. Readers are encouraged to use their discretion and judgment and consult with a qualified healthcare professional or nutritionist before making any significant changes to their diet, exercise, or lifestyle based on the information provided in this book.

The author and publisher make no guarantees about the results of any actions taken or decisions made based on the content of this book, and they are not liable for any losses, injuries, illnesses, or damages incurred by the user or any third party. The use of this information is at the sole discretion and risk of the reader.

Additionally, the author reserves the right to make changes, updates, or corrections to the content of this book in future versions, should they be deemed necessary to maintain accuracy and relevancy.

By reading and using the information in this book, readers acknowledge and agree to the terms of this disclaimer and legal notice. It is the responsibility of the reader to use the information provided responsibly and in accordance with applicable laws and regulations.

The Health Benefits of Smoothies
A Nutrient Powerhouse for Optimal Health and Vitality

Smoothies are nutritious powerhouses, giving us a plethora of advantages that contribute to our total well-being in a world where time is valuable and health is wealth. Smoothies have become popular because they are a quick and easy method to get a healthy dose of nutrients into your diet. Here are some of the reasons why drinking smoothies on a regular basis may dramatically improve your health:

Packed with essential nutrients:
Smoothies are a quick and simple method to get many nutrients into your body at once. A well-made smoothie may include a variety of nutrients important for general health, including vitamins, minerals, antioxidants, and fiber. The combination of fruits, veggies, and superfoods produces a strong mixture of nourishment that our bodies want.

Boosts immunity:
Having a strong immune system is essential for keeping disease at bay. Vitamin C and other antioxidants found in common smoothie components, including citrus fruits, berries, and leafy greens, help keep the body healthy and strong. Especially beneficial during the transition between seasons, regular ingestion can boost the body's defense systems and keep you healthy.

Supports Digestive Health:
Fiber is a superfood for your digestive system since it aids in digestion and helps you go to the bathroom more frequently. The fiber in common smoothie components like bananas, apples, and chia seeds promotes healthy digestion and a stronger digestive system. A healthy digestive tract is essential for taking in nutrients and feeling energized.

Aids in Weight Management:
If you're trying to lose weight, smoothies can be a great help. Their high fiber content makes you feel full while eating fewer calories. Greek yogurt and protein powder, both high in protein, are great additions to any meal or snack because they help you feel fuller for longer.

Hydration and Detoxification:
Several biological processes rely on enough water for their proper functioning. Smoothies help you stay hydrated since they contain liquids like water, coconut water, or herbal teas. In addition, the cleansing qualities of cucumbers and lemons help the body eliminate impurities and reveal healthy skin.

Energy Boost
Debilitating fatigue impairs performance and negatively impacts health. The

natural sugars, vitamins, and minerals included in fruits like bananas, mangoes, and berries make smoothies a healthy choice for a quick pick-me-up. They provide sustained energy and are a great option for before or after a workout.

Encourages healthy habits
Fruits and vegetables might be difficult to incorporate into one's diet for some people, but smoothies are a delicious alternative. You can customize the taste to your liking while still getting the nutrients you require by combining a wide range of ingredients.

Making smoothies a regular part of your diet is more than simply a matter of personal preference; it's a calculated move toward better health. If you want to be healthier and more energetic, drinking smoothies is a huge step in the right direction. Get out your blender, learn about the wondrous world of food, and set off on a tasty adventure toward health. Your body will express its gratitude by giving you renewed vigor, energy, and enthusiasm for life.

How to Make a Smoothie

Making a delicious smoothie requires skill and an appreciation for what goes into a well-balanced, savory blend.

Base Liquids: The building blocks of your smoothie are the base liquids you use. Water is flavorless; hence, it acts as a vehicle for other tastes. Coconut water adds a tropical twist that complements the inherent sweetness of any dish. Nut-rich almond milk and fragrant herbal teas make a delicious combination. Selecting an appropriate foundation improves both flavor and nutritional content, leading to a more personalized and satisfying eating experience.

Fruits and Vegetables: The flavor and health benefits of your smoothie may vary depending on the fruits and vegetables you use. Flavors from fresh fruits are lively, while those from frozen fruits are cool and rich. Strategically pairing fruits and vegetables can improve flavor harmony and boost nutritional synergy. This delicious and nutritious smoothie combines the tartness of berries with the earthiness of greens.

Proteins: Proteins are important since they aid in muscle recovery, keep you full, and keep your energy levels high. Greek yogurt is rich and protein-packed, while tofu is suitable for vegetarians. Add protein powders like whey, plant proteins, or collagen to your blend to help you reach your fitness objectives. You may make your smoothies a post-workout treat or a satisfying meal replacement by adjusting the amount and kind of protein included.

Healthy Fats: Add texture and nutrition to your smoothie by including healthy fats like avocado, almonds, and seeds. The avocados produce a rich, creamy texture, and the nuts and seeds add a pleasant crunch. These fats help you feel full longer, so you can enjoy your smoothie guilt-free. Your mix will taste even better when you add some healthy fats to the flavor profile.

Sweeteners and Flavor Enhancers: Natural sweeteners like honey, dates, or agave syrup can replace refined sugar in recipes without sacrificing flavor. Vanilla essence, cinnamon, and fresh herbs all improve flavor without adding unhealthy fats or sugars. To make a smoothie that is both healthy and delicious, you need to learn to balance the sweetness of your ingredients with the complexity of their flavors.

Secrets to Making the Best Smoothie Ever

This section is a goldmine of helpful information and insider tricks that will take your smoothie-making to the next level. Elevate your smoothie-making expertise with these indispensable tips, transforming your blends into culinary masterpieces.

Layering Methods: The sequence of adding ingredients impacts the blend's efficiency and smoothness. Layering strategically improves blending and guarantees a consistent texture. The order of preparation is liquids, then soft foods, then frozen or hard substances. This procedure guarantees an even mix that always results in a creamy texture that will satisfy your taste buds.

Preparation and Freezing: Frozen ingredients give your smoothie more body and chill. Add creaminess by freezing fruits like bananas, berries, or mango. You may save time mixing by prepping ingredients, including cutting up fruits and vegetables, ahead of time. With the ready-to-blend packets, your smoothie routine will be quick and easy.

Flavor Balancing: Finding that Sweet Spot is an Art Learn how to balance flavors by using sweet, sour, bitter, and salty flavors. Sweeten to taste with natural sugars, and counteract any bitterness with citrus or berries. Try pairing bitter ingredients, like kale, with sweet fruits. If your mix is too sweet or too sour, try adding some greens or citrus to balance the flavors.

Garnishing and Presentation: Improve your smoothie's presentation by getting creative with garnishes. The addition of fresh fruits, nuts, seeds, or edible flowers not only improves the dish's aesthetic appeal but also adds textural variety and depth of flavor. Try different combinations of garnishes to make a dish that's worthy of an Instagram post. Having your smoothie artfully decorated may make the entire experience of drinking it that much more enjoyable.

Know what to look out for so that your mixes come out perfectly every time. If the blender is overloaded, it won't be able to mix as well, and the results can be lumpy. Curdling or off tastes might occur if components aren't well-matched. By avoiding these errors, you may make smoothies reliably and deliciously every time, turning your experience into a thrilling and satisfying culinary adventure. You can make delicious smoothies if you know how to use the basic tools, have a firm grasp on the fundamental ingredients, and use expert techniques. This knowledge not only expands your gastronomic horizons but also improves your health and happiness, paving the way for a rich and rewarding life. Enjoy your mixing!

Tips for Health-Conscious Readers
Nourishing Your Body, Mind, and Soul

Variety is key. Use a variety of fruits, veggies, superfoods, and liquid bases in your experiments. If you want to receive a wide range of nutrients, it's best to use a wide range of colors in your meals.

Balance Your Ingredients: Make sure your smoothie has a good mix of healthy fats, protein, fiber, and complex carbs. Greek yogurt, nut butter, and plant-based protein powder are all great protein options to add to your diet.

Mindful Sweeteners: Instead of using refined sugar, try using a natural sweetener like honey, agave nectar, or dates. These sugar replacements are a healthy way to sweeten your smoothies without sacrificing taste or health benefits.

Prep in Advance: Make smoothie packets ahead of time and store them in the freezer. Pack materials by weight into freezer bags for later use. This is a time-saving measure that also guarantees a steady supply of nutritious food.

Add Greens: Smoothies are a great way to hide healthy vegetables like spinach, kale, and Swiss chard. As a result of their high vitamin, mineral, and antioxidant content, they improve the health benefits of your beverage without altering its flavor.

Boost with Superfoods: Increase the nutritional value of your smoothies by adding superfoods such as chia seeds, flaxseeds, spirulina, or acai powder. Adding these superfoods to your smoothies will increase their already substantial nutritional value.

Mind the Portions: Although smoothies are nutritious, it's important to watch how much of them you consume, especially if you're watching your calorie count. Try drinking your smoothies out of smaller cups and taking your time to relish each mouthful.

Hydration Matters: It's important to stay hydrated, so using a liquid base like water, coconut water, or herbal tea in your smoothies or shakes is a great idea. Maintaining an appropriate water intake is crucial to good health and peak bodily performance.

Pair with Whole Foods: Though delicious on their own, smoothies are best enjoyed in conjunction with a balanced, whole-food diet. Make smoothies a complement to your normal meals to increase your intake of healthy whole foods, including fruits, veggies, grains, and proteins.

Listen to Your Body: Pay Attention to Your System Watch how your body responds to various components. It's possible that some people have dietary sensitivities. If anything doesn't agree with you, play around with the ingredients until you find what does.

Maintain Consistency: Include Smoothies on a Regular Basis in Your Diet. The key to enjoying the long-term health advantages is consistency. Make a plan for when you'll eat, whether it's breakfast, a snack after exercise, or an afternoon pick-me-up.

Mindful Enjoyment: Practice mindful consumption by savoring every sip of your smoothie. Take this opportunity to really immerse yourself in the experience of something so nutritious as you eat. Thanksgiving for the healthy decisions you're making might increase when you practice mindful eating.

You may improve the health benefits of your smoothies and develop a more conscious relationship with your body if you follow these guidelines. Congratulations on your commitment to health and vitality!

ULTIMATE SMOOTHIE SENSATIONS

Recipe 1: Berry Blast Smoothie

Ingredients:
- 1 cup mixed berries (strawberries, blueberries, raspberries)
- 1 banana, peeled
- 1/2 cup Greek yogurt
- 1 tablespoon honey
- 1 cup almond milk
- Ice cubes (optional)

How to Prepare:
- Blend all the ingredients in a blender until smooth.
- Add ice cubes if desired.
- Serve immediately.

Recipe 2: Green Goddess Smoothie

Ingredients:
- 1 cup spinach leaves
- 1/2 cucumber, peeled and sliced
- 1/2 avocado, peeled and pitted
- 1 tablespoon chia seeds
- 1 tablespoon lemon juice
- 1 cup coconut water
- Ice cubes (optional)

How to Prepare:
- Combine all the ingredients in a blender.
- Blend until creamy and smooth.
- Add ice cubes if desired.
- Enjoy!

Recipe 3: Tropical Paradise Smoothie

Ingredients:
- 1/2 cup pineapple chunks
- 1/2 cup mango chunks
- 1 banana, peeled
- 1/2 cup coconut milk
- 1 tablespoon flax seeds
- 1 tablespoon honey
- Ice cubes (optional)

How to Prepare:
- Put all the ingredients into a blender.
- Blend until the mixture is smooth and creamy.
- Add ice cubes if desired. Serve immediately.

Recipe 4: Peanut Butter Power Smoothie

Ingredients:
- 2 tablespoons peanut butter
- 1 banana, peeled
- 1 cup milk (or almond milk for a dairy-free option)
- 1 tablespoon honey
- 1/2 teaspoon cinnamon powder
- Ice cubes (optional)

How to Prepare:
- Combine all the ingredients in a blender.
- Blend until the mixture is silky and lump-free.
- Add ice cubes if desired.
- Pour into a glass and enjoy!

Recipe 5: Citrus Sunshine Smoothie

Ingredients:
- 1 orange, peeled and segmented
- 1/2 grapefruit, peeled and segmented
- 1/2 cup plain yogurt
- 1 tablespoon honey
- 1/2 teaspoon vanilla extract
- Ice cubes (optional)

How to Prepare:
- Put all the ingredients into a blender.
- Blend until the mixture is smooth and creamy.
- Add ice cubes if desired.
- Serve immediately.

Recipe 6: Chocolate Banana Bliss Smoothie

Ingredients:
- 2 ripe bananas, peeled
- 2 tablespoons cocoa powder
- 1 tablespoon honey
- 1 cup milk (or almond milk for a dairy-free option)
- 1/2 teaspoon vanilla extract
- Ice cubes (optional)

How to Prepare:
- Combine all the ingredients in a blender.
- Blend until the mixture is velvety and chocolatey.
- Add ice cubes if desired.
- Pour into a glass and enjoy!

Recipe 7: Almond Joy Smoothie

Ingredients:
- 1/4 cup almonds, soaked and peeled
- 2 tablespoons shredded coconut
- 1 tablespoon cocoa powder
- 1 banana, peeled
- 1 cup almond milk
- 1 tablespoon honey
- Ice cubes (optional)

How to Prepare:
- Blend almonds, coconut, cocoa powder, banana, almond milk, and honey until smooth.
- Add ice cubes if desired.
- Blend again until the mixture is creamy.
- Serve and savor the taste of Almond Joy!

Recipe 8: Pomegranate Berry Burst Smoothie

Ingredients:
- 1/2 cup pomegranate seeds
- 1/2 cup strawberries, hulled
- 1/2 cup blueberries
- 1/2 cup plain yogurt
- 1 tablespoon honey
- 1/2 cup water
- Ice cubes (optional)

How to Prepare:
- Combine all the ingredients in a blender.
- Blend until the mixture is smooth and vibrant.
- Add ice cubes if desired.
- Pour into a glass and enjoy the burst of flavors!

Recipe 9: Spinach Mango Delight Smoothie

Ingredients:
- 1 cup spinach leaves
- 1 ripe mango, peeled and pitted
- 1/2 banana, peeled
- 1/2 cup coconut water
- 1 tablespoon chia seeds
- Ice cubes (optional)

How to Prepare:
- Put spinach, mango, banana, coconut water, and chia seeds in a

blender.
- Blend until the mixture is smooth and refreshing.
- Add ice cubes if desired.
- Serve immediately and relish the goodness of greens and mango!

Recipe 10: Avocado Mint Marvel Smoothie

Ingredients:
- 1/2 avocado, peeled and pitted
- 1 cup fresh mint leaves
- 1 tablespoon honey
- 1 tablespoon lime juice
- 1 cup almond milk
- Ice cubes (optional)

How to Prepare:
- Blend avocado, mint leaves, honey, lime juice, and almond milk until smooth.
- Add ice cubes if desired.
- Blend again until the mixture is creamy and minty.
- Pour into a glass and enjoy the refreshing Avocado Mint Marvel!

Recipe 11: Cherry Almond Bliss Smoothie

Ingredients:
- 1 cup cherries, pitted
- 1/4 cup almonds, soaked and peeled
- 1 cup almond milk
- 1 tablespoon honey
- 1/2 teaspoon almond extract
- Ice cubes (optional)

How to Prepare:
- Blend cherries, soaked almonds, almond milk, honey, and almond extract until smooth.
- Add ice cubes if desired.
- Blend again until creamy.
- Enjoy the delightful blend of cherries and almonds!

Recipe 12: Minty Pineapple Kale Smoothie

Ingredients:
- 1 cup pineapple chunks
- 1 cup kale leaves, stems removed
- 1/2 banana, peeled
- 1 tablespoon chia seeds

- 1 tablespoon fresh mint leaves
- 1 cup coconut water
- Ice cubes (optional)

How to Prepare:
- Combine pineapple, kale, banana, chia seeds, mint leaves, and coconut water in a blender.
- Blend until the mixture is smooth and vibrant.
- Add ice cubes if desired.
- Serve and enjoy the refreshing taste of mint and pineapple!

Recipe 13: Raspberry Lemonade Smoothie

Ingredients:
- 1 cup raspberries
- Juice of 2 lemons
- 1/2 cup plain yogurt
- 1 tablespoon honey
- 1 cup water
- Ice cubes (optional)

How to Prepare:
- Blend raspberries, lemon juice, yogurt, honey, and water until smooth.
- Add ice cubes if desired.
- Blend again until the mixture is frothy and tangy.
- Pour into a glass and savor the raspberry lemonade goodness!

Recipe 14: Oatmeal Cookie Smoothie

Ingredients:
- 1/2 cup rolled oats
- 1 tablespoon almond butter
- 1 ripe banana, peeled
- 1/2 teaspoon cinnamon powder
- 1 cup milk (or almond milk)
- 1 tablespoon honey
- Ice cubes (optional)

How to Prepare:
- Blend rolled oats, almond butter, banana, cinnamon, milk, and honey until smooth.
- Add ice cubes if desired.
- Blend again until the mixture is creamy and reminiscent of oatmeal cookies.
- Enjoy a guilt-free cookie-inspired smoothie!

Recipe 15: Carrot Cake Smoothie

Ingredients:
- 1 carrot, peeled and chopped
- 1/2 apple, cored and chopped
- 1/4 cup walnuts
- 1/2 teaspoon cinnamon powder
- 1 tablespoon honey
- 1 cup almond milk
- Ice cubes (optional)

How to Prepare:
- Blend carrot, apple, walnuts, cinnamon, honey, and almond milk until smooth.
- Add ice cubes if desired.
- Blend again until the mixture is velvety and reminiscent of carrot cake.
- Indulge in the flavors of a classic dessert in a healthy smoothie!

Recipe 16: Mango Basil Delight Smoothie

Ingredients:
- 1 ripe mango, peeled and pitted
- 1/2 cup fresh basil leaves
- Juice of 1 lime
- 1 tablespoon honey
- 1 cup coconut water
- Ice cubes (optional)

How to Prepare:
- Blend mango, basil leaves, lime juice, honey, and coconut water until smooth.
- Add ice cubes if desired.
- Blend again until the mixture is fragrant and refreshing.
- Enjoy the unique combination of mango and basil!

Recipe 17: Blueberry Bliss Smoothie

Ingredients:
- 1 cup blueberries
- 1/2 cup spinach leaves
- 1/2 banana, peeled
- 1 tablespoon chia seeds
- 1 cup almond milk
- 1 tablespoon honey
- Ice cubes (optional)

How to Prepare:
- Blend blueberries, spinach, banana, chia seeds, almond milk, and honey until smooth.
- Add ice cubes if desired.
- Blend again until the mixture is vibrant and luscious.
- Experience the blissful taste of blueberries!

Recipe 18: Peachy Keen Smoothie

Ingredients:
- 2 ripe peaches, peeled and pitted
- 1/2 cup plain yogurt
- 1 tablespoon honey
- 1/2 teaspoon vanilla extract
- 1 cup water
- Ice cubes (optional)

How to Prepare:
- Blend peaches, yogurt, honey, vanilla extract, and water until smooth.
- Add ice cubes if desired.
- Blend again until the mixture is creamy and peachy.
- Enjoy the natural sweetness of peaches in every sip!

Recipe 19: Cranberry Orange Zest Smoothie

Ingredients:
- 1 cup cranberries
- Juice of 2 oranges
- 1/2 teaspoon orange zest
- 1 tablespoon honey
- 1 cup coconut water
- Ice cubes (optional)

How to Prepare:
- Blend cranberries, orange juice, orange zest, honey, and coconut water until smooth.
- Add ice cubes if desired.
- Blend again until the mixture is zesty and refreshing.
- Experience the burst of cranberry and citrus flavors!

Recipe 20: Coconut Raspberry Dream Smoothie

Ingredients:
- 1/2 cup raspberries
- 1/2 cup coconut milk
- 1/4 cup shredded coconut
- 1 tablespoon honey
- 1/2 teaspoon vanilla extract
- Ice cubes (optional)

How to Prepare:
- Blend raspberries, coconut milk, shredded coconut, honey, and vanilla extract until smooth.
- Add ice cubes if desired.
- Blend again until the mixture is creamy and dreamy.
- Savor the tropical combination of coconut and raspberries!

Recipe 21: Matcha Green Tea Smoothie

Ingredients:
- 1 teaspoon matcha green tea powder
- 1 banana, peeled
- 1 cup spinach leaves
- 1 tablespoon honey
- 1 cup almond milk
- Ice cubes (optional)

How to Prepare:
- Blend matcha powder, banana, spinach, honey, and almond milk until smooth.
- Add ice cubes if desired.
- Blend again until the mixture is vibrant and energizing.
- Enjoy the antioxidant-rich goodness of matcha!

Recipe 22: Strawberry Shortcake Smoothie

Ingredients:
- 1 cup strawberries, hulled
- 1/2 cup oats
- 1/2 teaspoon vanilla extract
- 1 tablespoon honey
- 1 cup milk (or almond milk)
- Ice cubes (optional)

How to Prepare:
- Blend strawberries, oats, vanilla extract, honey, and milk until smooth.

- Add ice cubes if desired.
- Blend again until the mixture is creamy and reminiscent of strawberry shortcake.
- Indulge in the dessert-inspired delight!

Recipe 23: Spicy Mango Tango Smoothie

Ingredients:
- 1 ripe mango, peeled and pitted
- 1/2 teaspoon chili powder
- Juice of 1 lime
- 1 tablespoon honey
- 1 cup water
- Ice cubes (optional)

How to Prepare:
- Blend mango, chili powder, lime juice, honey, and water until smooth.
- Add ice cubes if desired.
- Blend again until the mixture is spicy, tangy, and refreshing.
- Experience the unique fusion of spice and sweetness!

Recipe 24: Banana Bread Smoothie

Ingredients:
- 2 ripe bananas, peeled
- 1/2 cup oats
- 1/2 teaspoon cinnamon powder
- 1 tablespoon almond butter
- 1 cup almond milk
- Ice cubes (optional)

How to Prepare:
- Blend bananas, oats, cinnamon powder, almond butter, and almond milk until smooth.
- Add ice cubes if desired.
- Blend again until the mixture is velvety and reminiscent of banana bread.
- Enjoy the flavors of freshly baked bread in a smoothie!

Recipe 25: Choco-Nut Heaven Smoothie

Ingredients:
- 2 tablespoons cocoa powder
- 2 tablespoons peanut butter
- 1 banana, peeled

- 1 cup almond milk
- 1 tablespoon honey
- Ice cubes (optional)

How to Prepare:
- Blend cocoa powder, peanut butter, banana, almond milk, and honey until smooth.
- Add ice cubes if desired.
- Blend again until the mixture is rich and chocolatey.
- Satisfy your chocolate cravings guilt-free!

Recipe 26: Vanilla Berry Swirl Smoothie

Ingredients:
- 1 cup mixed berries (strawberries, blueberries, raspberries)
- 1/2 teaspoon vanilla extract
- 1 tablespoon honey
- 1 cup Greek yogurt
- Ice cubes (optional)

How to Prepare:
- Blend mixed berries, vanilla extract, honey, and Greek yogurt until smooth.
- Add ice cubes if desired.
- Blend again until the mixture is swirled with berry goodness.
- Enjoy the delightful blend of vanilla and berries!

Recipe 27: Golden Turmeric Elixir Smoothie

Ingredients:
- 1 teaspoon turmeric powder
- 1/2 teaspoon ginger powder
- 1 banana, peeled
- 1 tablespoon honey
- 1 cup coconut milk
- Ice cubes (optional)

How to Prepare:
- Blend turmeric powder, ginger powder, banana, honey, and coconut milk until smooth.
- Add ice cubes if desired.
- Blend again until the mixture is golden and invigorating.
- Experience the health benefits of turmeric in a delicious way!

Recipe 28: Raspberry Chocolate Indulgence Smoothie

Ingredients:
- 1 cup raspberries
- 2 tablespoons cocoa powder
- 1 tablespoon honey
- 1 cup almond milk
- Ice cubes (optional)

How to Prepare:
- Blend raspberries, cocoa powder, honey, and almond milk until smooth.
- Add ice cubes if desired.
- Blend again until the mixture is decadent and indulgent.
- Treat yourself to a guilt-free chocolate indulgence!

Recipe 29: Pina Colada Paradise Smoothie

Ingredients:
- 1/2 cup pineapple chunks
- 1/2 cup coconut milk
- 1/4 cup shredded coconut
- 1 tablespoon honey
- 1/2 teaspoon vanilla extract
- Ice cubes (optional)

How to Prepare:
- Blend pineapple chunks, coconut milk, shredded coconut, honey, and vanilla extract until smooth.
- Add ice cubes if desired.
- Blend again until the mixture is tropical and heavenly.
- Transport yourself to a paradise with every sip!

Recipe 30: Detox Green Smoothie

Ingredients:
- 1 cup kale leaves, stems removed
- 1/2 cucumber, peeled and sliced
- Juice of 1 lemon
- 1 tablespoon chia seeds
- 1 tablespoon fresh parsley leaves
- 1 cup coconut water
- Ice cubes (optional)

How to Prepare:
- Blend kale, cucumber, lemon juice, chia seeds, parsley leaves, and coconut water until smooth.

- Add ice cubes if desired.
- Blend again until the mixture is refreshing and detoxifying.
- Cleanse your body with this nourishing green smoothie!

Recipe 31: Mint Chocolate Chip Smoothie

Ingredients:
- 1 cup spinach leaves
- 1 tablespoon cocoa powder
- 1/2 teaspoon peppermint extract
- 1 tablespoon honey
- 1 cup almond milk
- Ice cubes (optional)

How to Prepare:
- Blend spinach, cocoa powder, peppermint extract, honey, and almond milk until smooth.
- Add ice cubes if desired.
- Blend again until the mixture is creamy and reminiscent of mint chocolate chip ice cream.
- Indulge in a guilt-free chocolate treat!

Recipe 32: Sweet Potato Pie Smoothie

Ingredients:
- 1/2 cup cooked and mashed sweet potato
- 1/2 teaspoon cinnamon powder
- 1 tablespoon maple syrup
- 1 cup almond milk
- 1/4 teaspoon nutmeg
- Ice cubes (optional)

How to Prepare:
- Blend sweet potato, cinnamon powder, maple syrup, almond milk, and nutmeg until smooth.
- Add ice cubes if desired.
- Blend again until the mixture is velvety and tastes like sweet potato pie.
- Enjoy the flavors of fall in a glass!

Recipe 33: Cucumber Melon Cooler Smoothie

Ingredients:
- 1/2 cucumber, peeled and sliced
- 1 cup honeydew melon chunks
- Juice of 1 lime

- 1 tablespoon honey
- 1 cup coconut water
- Ice cubes (optional)

How to Prepare:
- Blend cucumber, honeydew melon, lime juice, honey, and coconut water until smooth.
- Add ice cubes if desired.
- Blend again until the mixture is refreshing and cooling.
- Stay hydrated with this revitalizing smoothie!

Recipe 34: Pistachio Paradise Smoothie

Ingredients:
- 1/4 cup shelled pistachios
- 1/2 banana, peeled
- 1 cup spinach leaves
- 1 tablespoon honey
- 1 cup almond milk
- Ice cubes (optional)

How to Prepare:
- Blend pistachios, banana, spinach, honey, and almond milk until smooth.
- Add ice cubes if desired.
- Blend again until the mixture is creamy and nutty.
- Experience the unique taste of pistachios in a smoothie!

Recipe 35: Mango Ginger Zinger Smoothie

Ingredients:
- 1 ripe mango, peeled and pitted
- 1/2 teaspoon freshly grated ginger
- Juice of 1 orange
- 1 tablespoon honey
- 1 cup coconut water
- Ice cubes (optional)

How to Prepare:
- Blend mango, grated ginger, orange juice, honey, and coconut water until smooth.
- Add ice cubes if desired.
- Blend again until the mixture is zesty and invigorating.
- Boost your immune system with this mango ginger delight!

Recipe 36: **Raspberry Avocado Refresher Smoothie**

Ingredients:
- 1/2 cup raspberries
- 1/2 avocado, peeled and pitted
- 1 tablespoon honey
- 1 tablespoon lemon juice
- 1 cup almond milk
- Ice cubes (optional)

How to Prepare:
- Blend raspberries, avocado, honey, lemon juice, and almond milk until smooth.
- Add ice cubes if desired.
- Blend again until the mixture is creamy and refreshing.
- Enjoy the creamy texture of avocado with the tartness of raspberries!

Recipe 37: Cherry **Chocolate** Delight Smoothie

Ingredients:
- 1 cup cherries, pitted
- 2 tablespoons cocoa powder
- 1 tablespoon honey
- 1 cup almond milk
- Ice cubes (optional)

How to Prepare:
- Blend cherries, cocoa powder, honey, and almond milk until smooth.
- Add ice cubes if desired.
- Blend again until the mixture is rich and indulgent.
- Experience the heavenly combination of cherries and chocolate!

Recipe 38: **Pomegranate** Green Tea Boost Smoothie

Ingredients:
- 1/2 cup pomegranate seeds
- 1 teaspoon green tea powder
- 1 tablespoon honey
- 1 cup spinach leaves
- 1 cup water
- Ice cubes (optional)

How to Prepare:
- Blend pomegranate seeds, green tea powder, honey, spinach, and water until smooth.

- Add ice cubes if desired.
- Blend again until the mixture is antioxidant-rich and revitalizing.
- Enjoy the benefits of green tea in a fruity smoothie!

Recipe 39: **Blackberry Basil Bliss Smoothie**

Ingredients:
- 1 cup blackberries
- 1/4 cup fresh basil leaves
- Juice of 1 lemon
- 1 tablespoon honey
- 1 cup coconut water
- Ice cubes (optional)

How to Prepare:
- Blend blackberries, basil leaves, lemon juice, honey, and coconut water until smooth.
- Add ice cubes if desired.
- Blend again until the mixture is fragrant and refreshing.
- Experience the unique blend of blackberries and basil!

Recipe 40: Carrot Cake Detox Smoothie

Ingredients:
- 1 carrot, peeled and chopped
- 1/2 apple, cored and chopped
- 1/4 cup walnuts
- 1/2 teaspoon cinnamon powder
- 1 tablespoon chia seeds
- 1 cup coconut water
- Ice cubes (optional)

How to Prepare:
- Blend carrot, apple, walnuts, cinnamon powder, chia seeds, and coconut water until smooth.
- Add ice cubes if desired.
- Blend again until the mixture is creamy and reminiscent of carrot cake.
- Cleanse your body with the flavors of carrot cake!

Recipe 41: Mango Turmeric Tango Smoothie

Ingredients:
- 1 ripe mango, peeled and pitted
- 1/2 teaspoon turmeric powder
- 1 tablespoon honey

- 1 cup almond milk
- 1/2 teaspoon vanilla extract
- Ice cubes (optional)

How to Prepare:
- Blend mango, turmeric powder, honey, almond milk, and vanilla extract until smooth.
- Add ice cubes if desired.
- Blend again until the mixture is golden and exotic.
- Enjoy the tropical twist of mango and turmeric!

Recipe 42: Cherry Almond Spinach Smoothie

Ingredients:
- 1 cup cherries, pitted
- 1/4 cup almonds, soaked and peeled
- 1 cup spinach leaves
- 1 tablespoon honey
- 1 cup coconut water
- Ice cubes (optional)

How to Prepare:
- Blend cherries, almonds, spinach, honey, and coconut water until smooth.
- Add ice cubes if desired.
- Blend again until the mixture is creamy and packed with nutrients.
- Savor the combination of cherries, almonds, and spinach!

Recipe 43: Papaya Passion Smoothie

Ingredients:
- 1 cup papaya chunks
- Juice of 1 lime
- 1 tablespoon honey
- 1 cup coconut water
- 1/2 teaspoon vanilla extract
- Ice cubes (optional)

How to Prepare:
- Blend papaya chunks, lime juice, honey, coconut water, and vanilla extract until smooth.
- Add ice cubes if desired.
- Blend again until the mixture is tropical and invigorating.
- Experience the passion of papaya in every sip!

Recipe 44: Berry Basil Blast Smoothie

Ingredients:
- 1 cup mixed berries (strawberries, blueberries, raspberries)
- 1/4 cup fresh basil leaves
- 1 tablespoon honey
- 1 cup Greek yogurt
- 1/2 teaspoon lemon zest
- Ice cubes (optional)

How to Prepare:
- Blend mixed berries, basil leaves, honey, Greek yogurt, and lemon zest until smooth.
- Add ice cubes if desired.
- Blend again until the mixture is vibrant and refreshing.
- Enjoy the unique blend of berries and basil!

Recipe 45: Cantaloupe Cooler Smoothie

Ingredients:
- 1 cup cantaloupe chunks
- 1/2 cup cucumber, peeled and sliced
- Juice of 1 orange
- 1 tablespoon honey
- 1 cup coconut water
- Ice cubes (optional)

How to Prepare:
- Blend cantaloupe chunks, cucumber, orange juice, honey, and coconut water until smooth.
- Add ice cubes if desired.
- Blend again until the mixture is cooling and revitalizing.
- Stay refreshed with this hydrating smoothie!

Recipe 46: Peach Basil Breeze Smoothie

Ingredients:
- 2 ripe peaches, peeled and pitted
- 1/4 cup fresh basil leaves
- 1 tablespoon honey
- 1 cup almond milk
- 1/2 teaspoon vanilla extract
- Ice cubes (optional)

How to Prepare:
- Blend peaches, basil leaves, honey, almond milk, and vanilla extract until smooth.

- Add ice cubes if desired.
- Blend again until the mixture is peachy and aromatic.
- Enjoy the soothing blend of peaches and basil!

Recipe 47: Blueberry Lavender Dream Smoothie

Ingredients:
- 1 cup blueberries
- 1/2 teaspoon dried lavender buds
- 1 tablespoon honey
- 1 cup almond milk
- 1/2 teaspoon vanilla extract
- Ice cubes (optional)

How to Prepare:
- Blend blueberries, lavender buds, honey, almond milk, and vanilla extract until smooth.
- Add ice cubes if desired.
- Blend again until the mixture is fragrant and dreamy.
- Experience the calming effect of lavender with the sweetness of blueberries!

Recipe 48: Raspberry Rose Elixir Smoothie

Ingredients:
- 1 cup raspberries
- 1/2 teaspoon rose water
- 1 tablespoon honey
- 1 cup coconut water
- Juice of 1/2 lemon
- Ice cubes (optional)

How to Prepare:
- Blend raspberries, rose water, honey, coconut water, and lemon juice until smooth.
- Add ice cubes if desired.
- Blend again until the mixture is floral and delightful.
- Enjoy the romantic fusion of raspberries and rose water!

Recipe 49: Ginger Pear Spice Smoothie

Ingredients:
- 1 ripe pear, peeled and chopped
- 1/2 teaspoon freshly grated ginger
- 1/2 teaspoon cinnamon powder
- 1 tablespoon honey

ULTIMATE SMOOTHIE SENSATIONS

- 1 cup almond milk
- Ice cubes (optional)

How to Prepare:
- Blend pear, ginger, cinnamon powder, honey, and almond milk until smooth.
- Add ice cubes if desired.
- Blend again until the mixture is warming and comforting.
- Experience the spicy sweetness of ginger and cinnamon!

Recipe 50: Coconut Berry Bliss Smoothie

Ingredients:
- 1/2 cup mixed berries (strawberries, blueberries, raspberries)
- 1/2 cup coconut milk
- 1 tablespoon honey
- 1/4 cup shredded coconut
- 1 cup coconut water
- Ice cubes (optional)

How to Prepare:
- Blend mixed berries, coconut milk, honey, shredded coconut, and coconut water until smooth.
- Add ice cubes if desired.
- Blend again until the mixture is tropical and blissful.
- Indulge in the coconutty goodness of this refreshing smoothie!

Recipe 51: Pineapple Ginger Zing Smoothie

Ingredients:
- 1 cup pineapple chunks
- 1/2 teaspoon freshly grated ginger
- 1 tablespoon honey
- 1 cup coconut water
- Juice of 1/2 lime
- Ice cubes (optional)

How to Prepare:
- Blend pineapple chunks, ginger, honey, coconut water, and lime juice until smooth.
- Add ice cubes if desired.
- Blend again until the mixture is zesty and refreshing.
- Experience the invigorating combination of pineapple and ginger!

Recipe 52: Vanilla Fig Delight Smoothie

Ingredients:
- 2 ripe figs, stems removed and chopped
- 1/2 teaspoon vanilla extract
- 1 tablespoon honey
- 1 cup almond milk
- 1/4 teaspoon cinnamon powder
- Ice cubes (optional)

How to Prepare:
- Blend figs, vanilla extract, honey, almond milk, and cinnamon powder until smooth.
- Add ice cubes if desired.
- Blend again until the mixture is velvety and indulgent.
- Enjoy the luxurious taste of vanilla and figs!

Recipe 53: Minty Watermelon Refresher Smoothie

Ingredients:
- 2 cups watermelon chunks, seeds removed
- 1/4 cup fresh mint leaves
- Juice of 1/2 lemon
- 1 tablespoon honey
- 1 cup coconut water
- Ice cubes (optional)

How to Prepare:
- Blend watermelon chunks, mint leaves, lemon juice, honey, and coconut water until smooth.
- Add ice cubes if desired.
- Blend again until the mixture is cool and revitalizing.
- Stay hydrated with this minty watermelon delight!

Recipe 54: Cacao Berry Protein Boost Smoothie

Ingredients:
- 1 cup mixed berries (strawberries, blueberries, raspberries)
- 2 tablespoons cocoa powder
- 1 scoop vanilla protein powder
- 1 tablespoon honey
- 1 cup almond milk
- Ice cubes (optional)

How to Prepare:
- Blend mixed berries, cocoa powder, protein powder, honey, and

almond milk until smooth.
- Add ice cubes if desired.
- Blend again until the mixture is rich and protein-packed.
- Energize your day with this berry-chocolate protein boost!

Recipe 55: Chia Cherry Chiller Smoothie

Ingredients:
- 1 cup cherries, pitted
- 1 tablespoon chia seeds
- 1 tablespoon honey
- 1 cup coconut water
- Juice of 1/2 lime
- Ice cubes (optional)

How to Prepare:
- Blend cherries, chia seeds, honey, coconut water, and lime juice until smooth.
- Add ice cubes if desired.
- Blend again until the mixture is hydrating and satisfying.
- Enjoy the texture of chia seeds in this cherry chiller!

Recipe 56: Spirulina Blueberry Blast Smoothie

Ingredients:
- 1 cup blueberries
- 1 teaspoon spirulina powder
- 1 tablespoon honey
- 1 cup almond milk
- 1/2 teaspoon vanilla extract
- Ice cubes (optional)

How to Prepare:
- Blend blueberries, spirulina powder, honey, almond milk, and vanilla extract until smooth.
- Add ice cubes if desired.
- Blend again until the mixture is vibrant and packed with nutrients.
- Boost your day with this spirulina-powered smoothie!

Recipe 57: Raspberry Lemon Verbena Smoothie

Ingredients:
- 1 cup raspberries
- 1 tablespoon fresh lemon verbena leaves
- Juice of 1 lemon

- 1 tablespoon honey
- 1 cup coconut water
- Ice cubes (optional)

How to Prepare:
- Blend raspberries, lemon verbena leaves, lemon juice, honey, and coconut water until smooth.
- Add ice cubes if desired.
- Blend again until the mixture is fragrant and revitalizing.
- Experience the unique flavor of lemon verbena with raspberries!

Recipe 58: Turmeric Mango Sunrise Smoothie

Ingredients:
- 1 ripe mango, peeled and pitted
- 1/2 teaspoon turmeric powder
- 1 tablespoon honey
- 1 cup almond milk
- 1/2 teaspoon orange zest
- Ice cubes (optional)

How to Prepare:
- Blend mango, turmeric powder, honey, almond milk, and orange zest until smooth.
- Add ice cubes if desired.
- Blend again until the mixture is golden and energizing.
- Start your day with this turmeric mango delight!

Recipe 59: Blackberry Sage Infusion Smoothie

Ingredients:
- 1 cup blackberries
- 1 tablespoon fresh sage leaves
- 1 tablespoon honey
- 1 cup almond milk
- Juice of 1/2 lemon
- Ice cubes (optional)

How to Prepare:
- Blend blackberries, sage leaves, honey, almond milk, and lemon juice until smooth.
- Add ice cubes if desired.
- Blend again until the mixture is aromatic and refreshing.
- Enjoy the herbal essence of sage with blackberries!

Recipe 60: Coconut Kiwi Kale Kick Smoothie

Ingredients:
- 2 kiwis, peeled and sliced
- 1/2 cup kale leaves, stems removed
- 1/2 cup coconut milk
- 1 tablespoon honey
- Juice of 1/2 lime
- Ice cubes (optional)

How to Prepare:
- Blend kiwis, kale leaves, coconut milk, honey, and lime juice until smooth.
- Add ice cubes if desired.
- Blend again until the mixture is tropical and revitalizing.
- Get a kick of energy with this coconut kiwi kale smoothie!

Recipe 61: Mango Matcha Madness Smoothie

Ingredients:
- 1 ripe mango, peeled and pitted
- 1 teaspoon matcha green tea powder
- 1 tablespoon honey
- 1 cup almond milk
- Ice cubes (optional)

How to Prepare:
- Blend mango, matcha powder, honey, and almond milk until smooth.
- Add ice cubes if desired.
- Blend again until the mixture is vibrant and energizing.
- Enjoy the perfect fusion of mango sweetness and matcha goodness!

Recipe 62: Chocolate Raspberry Love Smoothie

Ingredients:
- 1 cup raspberries
- 2 tablespoons cocoa powder
- 1 tablespoon honey
- 1 cup almond milk
- Ice cubes (optional)

How to Prepare:
- Blend raspberries, cocoa powder, honey, and almond milk until smooth. Add ice cubes if desired.
- Blend again until the mixture is rich and indulgent.
- Experience the romantic combination of chocolate and raspberries!

Recipe 63: Peachy Green Goddess Smoothie

Ingredients:
- 2 ripe peaches, peeled and pitted
- 1 cup spinach leaves
- 1/2 cucumber, peeled and sliced
- 1 tablespoon honey
- 1 cup coconut water
- Ice cubes (optional)

How to Prepare:
- Blend peaches, spinach, cucumber, honey, and coconut water until smooth.
- Add ice cubes if desired.
- Blend again until the mixture is refreshing and green.
- Embrace the goddess of health with this green smoothie!

Recipe 64: Blueberry Lavender Lemonade Smoothie

Ingredients:
- 1 cup blueberries
- 1/2 teaspoon dried lavender buds
- Juice of 1 lemon
- 1 tablespoon honey
- 1 cup coconut water
- Ice cubes (optional)

How to Prepare:
- Blend blueberries, lavender buds, lemon juice, honey, and coconut water until smooth.
- Add ice cubes if desired.
- Blend again until the mixture is fragrant and reminiscent of lavender lemonade.
- Enjoy the calming effect of lavender with the zest of lemon!

Recipe 65: Banana Nut Bread Smoothie

Ingredients:
- 2 ripe bananas, peeled
- 1/4 cup walnuts
- 1/2 teaspoon cinnamon powder
- 1 tablespoon honey
- 1 cup almond milk
- Ice cubes (optional)

How to Prepare:
- Blend bananas, walnuts, cinnamon powder, honey, and almond milk until smooth.
- Add ice cubes if desired.
- Blend again until the mixture is creamy and reminiscent of banana nut bread.
- Indulge in the comforting flavors of this smoothie!

Recipe 66: Cucumber Mint Cooler Smoothie

Ingredients:
- 1/2 cucumber, peeled and sliced
- 1/4 cup fresh mint leaves
- Juice of 1 lime
- 1 tablespoon honey
- 1 cup coconut water
- Ice cubes (optional)

How to Prepare:
- Blend cucumber, mint leaves, lime juice, honey, and coconut water until smooth.
- Add ice cubes if desired.
- Blend again until the mixture is cool and revitalizing.
- Stay refreshed with this hydrating cucumber mint smoothie!

Recipe 67: Mocha Almond Dream Smoothie

Ingredients:
- 1 tablespoon cocoa powder
- 2 tablespoons almond butter
- 1 tablespoon honey
- 1 cup almond milk
- 1 shot of espresso (optional)
- Ice cubes (optional)

How to Prepare:
- Blend cocoa powder, almond butter, honey, almond milk, and espresso (if using) until smooth.
- Add ice cubes if desired.
- Blend again until the mixture is rich and indulgent.
- Satisfy your coffee and chocolate cravings in one delightful sip!

Recipe 68: Mango Pineapple Paradise Smoothie

Ingredients:
- 1 ripe mango, peeled and pitted
- 1 cup pineapple chunks
- 1 tablespoon honey
- 1 cup coconut milk
- Ice cubes (optional)

How to Prepare:
- Blend mango, pineapple chunks, honey, and coconut milk until smooth.
- Add ice cubes if desired.
- Blend again until the mixture is tropical and heavenly.
- Transport yourself to a paradise with this mango pineapple delight!

Recipe 69: Raspberry Coconut Crush Smoothie

Ingredients:
- 1 cup raspberries
- 1/2 cup coconut milk
- 1 tablespoon honey
- 1/4 cup shredded coconut
- 1 cup coconut water
- Ice cubes (optional)

How to Prepare:
- Blend raspberries, coconut milk, honey, shredded coconut, and coconut water until smooth.
- Add ice cubes if desired.
- Blend again until the mixture is creamy and coconutty.
- Enjoy the refreshing raspberry coconut combination!

Recipe 70: Green Tea Mango Zen Smoothie

Ingredients:
- 1 ripe mango, peeled and pitted
- 1 teaspoon green tea powder
- 1 tablespoon honey
- 1 cup almond milk
- 1/2 teaspoon vanilla extract
- Ice cubes (optional)

How to Prepare:
- Blend mango, green tea powder, honey, almond milk, and vanilla extract until smooth.

- Add ice cubes if desired.
- Blend again until the mixture is soothing and zen-like.
- Enjoy the calming blend of green tea and mango!

Recipe 71: Papaya Passionflower Bliss Smoothie

Ingredients:
- 1 cup papaya chunks
- 1 tablespoon passionflower tea leaves (brewed and cooled)
- 1 tablespoon honey
- 1 cup coconut water
- Juice of 1/2 lime
- Ice cubes (optional)

How to Prepare:
- Blend papaya chunks, cooled passionflower tea, honey, coconut water, and lime juice until smooth.
- Add ice cubes if desired.
- Blend again until the mixture is exotic and refreshing.
- Enjoy the calming effects of passionflower with the sweetness of papaya!

Recipe 72: Apricot Almond Sunrise Smoothie

Ingredients:
- 1 cup apricot halves, pitted
- 2 tablespoons almond butter
- 1 tablespoon honey
- 1 cup almond milk
- 1/2 teaspoon vanilla extract
- Ice cubes (optional)

How to Prepare:
- Blend apricot halves, almond butter, honey, almond milk, and vanilla extract until smooth.
- Add ice cubes if desired.
- Blend again until the mixture is creamy and reminiscent of a sunny morning.
- Start your day with this apricot almond delight!

Recipe 73: **Strawberry Basil Infusion Smoothie**

Ingredients:
- 1 cup strawberries, hulled
- 1/4 cup fresh basil leaves
- 1 tablespoon honey
- 1 cup coconut water
- Juice of 1/2 lemon
- Ice cubes (optional)

How to Prepare:
- Blend strawberries, basil leaves, honey, coconut water, and lemon juice until smooth.
- Add ice cubes if desired.
- Blend again until the mixture is fragrant and revitalizing.
- Experience the unique blend of strawberries and basil!

Recipe 74: Minty **Pineapple Cooler Smoothie**

Ingredients:
- 1 cup pineapple chunks
- 1/4 cup fresh mint leaves
- Juice of 1 lime
- 1 tablespoon honey
- 1 cup coconut water
- Ice cubes (optional)

How to Prepare:
- Blend pineapple chunks, mint leaves, lime juice, honey, and coconut water until smooth.
- Add ice cubes if desired.
- Blend again until the mixture is cool and refreshing.
- Stay hydrated with this minty pineapple delight!

Recipe 75: **Raspberry Hibiscus Harmony Smoothie**

Ingredients:
- 1 cup raspberries
- 1 tablespoon dried hibiscus petals (brewed and cooled)
- 1 tablespoon honey
- 1 cup coconut water
- Juice of 1/2 orange
- Ice cubes (optional)

How to Prepare:
- Blend raspberries, cooled hibiscus tea, honey, coconut water, and

orange juice until smooth.
- Add ice cubes if desired.
- Blend again until the mixture is floral and harmonious.
- Enjoy the soothing blend of raspberries and hibiscus!

Recipe 76: Goji Berry Citrus Boost Smoothie

Ingredients:
- 1/2 cup goji berries (soaked in water and drained)
- Juice of 2 oranges
- 1 tablespoon honey
- 1 cup coconut water
- 1/2 teaspoon grated orange zest
- Ice cubes (optional)

How to Prepare:
- Blend soaked goji berries, orange juice, honey, coconut water, and orange zest until smooth.
- Add ice cubes if desired.
- Blend again until the mixture is citrusy and energizing.
- Boost your day with this goji berry citrus delight!

Recipe 77: Cherry Vanilla Serenity Smoothie

Ingredients:
- 1 cup cherries, pitted
- 1/2 teaspoon vanilla extract
- 1 tablespoon honey
- 1 cup almond milk
- 1/4 teaspoon almond extract
- Ice cubes (optional)

How to Prepare:
- Blend cherries, vanilla extract, honey, almond milk, and almond extract until smooth.
- Add ice cubes if desired.
- Blend again until the mixture is creamy and serene.
- Enjoy the comforting blend of cherries and vanilla!

Recipe 78: Ginger Pear Immunity Boost Smoothie

Ingredients:
- 1 ripe pear, peeled and chopped
- 1/2 teaspoon freshly grated ginger
- Juice of 1 lemon
- 1 tablespoon honey

- 1 cup coconut water
- Ice cubes (optional)

How to Prepare:
- Blend pear, ginger, lemon juice, honey, coconut water until smooth.
- Add ice cubes if desired.
- Blend again until the mixture is immune-boosting and refreshing.
- Support your immunity with this ginger pear delight!

Recipe 79: Figgy Blueberry Bliss Smoothie

Ingredients:
- 2 ripe figs, stems removed and chopped
- 1 cup blueberries
- 1 tablespoon honey
- 1 cup almond milk
- 1/2 teaspoon cinnamon powder
- Ice cubes (optional)

How to Prepare:
- Blend figs, blueberries, honey, almond milk, and cinnamon powder until smooth.
- Add ice cubes if desired.
- Blend again until the mixture is creamy and blissful.
- Enjoy the luxurious blend of figs and blueberries!

Recipe 80: Banana Cocoa Crunch Smoothie

Ingredients:
- 2 ripe bananas, peeled
- 2 tablespoons cocoa powder
- 1 tablespoon honey
- 1 cup almond milk
- 1/4 cup granola
- Ice cubes (optional)

How to Prepare:
- Blend bananas, cocoa powder, honey, and almond milk until smooth.
- Add ice cubes if desired.
- Blend again until the mixture is rich and chocolatey.
- Top with granola for a delightful crunch!

Recipe 81: Avocado Mint Chocolate Chip Smoothie

Ingredients:
- 1/2 ripe avocado, peeled and pitted
- 1 tablespoon cocoa nibs or cocoa powder
- 1/4 cup fresh mint leaves
- 1 tablespoon honey
- 1 cup almond milk
- Ice cubes (optional)

How to Prepare:
- Blend avocado, cocoa nibs, mint leaves, honey, and almond milk until smooth.
- Add ice cubes if desired.
- Blend again until the mixture is creamy and indulgent.
- Enjoy the rich flavors of chocolate and mint with the goodness of avocado!

Recipe 82: Raspberry Mango Basil Bliss Smoothie

Ingredients:
- 1 cup raspberries
- 1 ripe mango, peeled and pitted
- 1/4 cup fresh basil leaves
- 1 tablespoon honey
- 1 cup coconut water
- Ice cubes (optional)

How to Prepare:
- Blend raspberries, mango, basil leaves, honey, and coconut water until smooth.
- Add ice cubes if desired.
- Blend again until the mixture is fragrant and refreshing.
- Experience the delightful combination of raspberry, mango, and basil!

Recipe 83: Spinach Pineapple Paradise Smoothie

Ingredients:
- 1 cup spinach leaves
- 1 cup pineapple chunks
- 1 tablespoon honey
- 1/2 teaspoon grated ginger
- 1 cup coconut water
- Ice cubes (optional)

How to Prepare:
- Blend spinach leaves, pineapple chunks, honey, grated ginger, and coconut water until smooth.
- Add ice cubes if desired.
- Blend again until the mixture is tropical and revitalizing.
- Enjoy the nutrient-packed goodness of spinach and pineapple!

Recipe 84: Blueberry Coconut Chia Smoothie

Ingredients:
- 1 cup blueberries
- 1/2 cup coconut milk
- 1 tablespoon chia seeds
- 1 tablespoon honey
- 1 cup coconut water
- Ice cubes (optional)

How to Prepare:
- Blend blueberries, coconut milk, chia seeds, honey, and coconut water until smooth.
- Add ice cubes if desired.
- Blend again until the mixture is thick and satisfying.
- Embrace the texture of chia seeds in this blueberry coconut delight!

Recipe 85: Peach Raspberry Rose Smoothie

Ingredients:
- 2 ripe peaches, peeled and pitted
- 1 cup raspberries
- 1/2 teaspoon rose water
- 1 tablespoon honey
- 1 cup almond milk
- Ice cubes (optional)

How to Prepare:
- Blend peaches, raspberries, rose water, honey, and almond milk until smooth.
- Add ice cubes if desired.
- Blend again until the mixture is floral and delightful.
- Experience the romantic fusion of peaches, raspberries, and rose water!

Recipe 86: Cucumber Kiwi Kale Crush Smoothie

Ingredients:
- 1/2 cucumber, peeled and sliced
- 2 kiwis, peeled and sliced
- 1/2 cup kale leaves, stems removed
- 1 tablespoon honey
- 1 cup coconut water
- Ice cubes (optional)

How to Prepare:
- Blend cucumber, kiwis, kale leaves, honey, and coconut water until smooth.
- Add ice cubes if desired.
- Blend again until the mixture is refreshing and green.
- Enjoy the hydrating blend of cucumber, kiwi, and kale!

Recipe 87: Mango Pine Nut Euphoria Smoothie

Ingredients:
- 1 ripe mango, peeled and pitted
- 2 tablespoons pine nuts
- 1 tablespoon honey
- 1 cup almond milk
- 1/2 teaspoon cardamom powder
- Ice cubes (optional)

How to Prepare:
- Blend mango, pine nuts, honey, almond milk, and cardamom powder until smooth.
- Add ice cubes if desired.
- Blend again until the mixture is creamy and euphoric.
- Indulge in the delightful crunch of pine nuts with the sweetness of mango!

Recipe 88: Orange Carrot Turmeric Twist Smoothie

Ingredients:
- 2 oranges, peeled and segmented
- 1 carrot, peeled and chopped
- 1/2 teaspoon turmeric powder
- 1 tablespoon honey
- 1 cup coconut water
- Ice cubes (optional)

How to Prepare:
- Blend oranges, carrot, turmeric powder, honey, and coconut water until smooth.
- Add ice cubes if desired.
- Blend again until the mixture is vibrant and invigorating.
- Enjoy the citrusy twist with the goodness of carrots and turmeric!

Recipe 89: Mixed Berry Maca Magic Smoothie

Ingredients:
- 1/2 cup mixed berries (strawberries, blueberries, raspberries)
- 1 teaspoon maca powder
- 1 tablespoon honey
- 1 cup almond milk
- 1/2 teaspoon vanilla extract
- Ice cubes (optional)

How to Prepare:
- Blend mixed berries, maca powder, honey, almond milk, and vanilla extract until smooth.
- Add ice cubes if desired.
- Blend again until the mixture is energizing and magical.
- Boost your vitality with this mixed berry maca delight!

Recipe 90: Coconut Mango Macadamia Smoothie

Ingredients:
- 1 ripe mango, peeled and pitted
- 1/4 cup macadamia nuts
- 1/2 cup coconut milk
- 1 tablespoon honey
- 1 cup coconut water
- Ice cubes (optional)

How to Prepare:
- Blend mango, macadamia nuts, coconut milk, honey, and coconut water until smooth.
- Add ice cubes if desired.
- Blend again until the mixture is creamy and tropical.
- Experience the nutty crunch of macadamia with the sweetness of mango!

Recipe 91: Pomegranate Berry Burst Smoothie

Ingredients:
- 1/2 cup pomegranate seeds
- 1/2 cup strawberries, hulled
- 1/2 cup blueberries
- 1 tablespoon honey
- 1 cup coconut water
- Ice cubes (optional)

How to Prepare:
- Blend pomegranate seeds, strawberries, blueberries, honey, and coconut water until smooth.
- Add ice cubes if desired.
- Blend again until the mixture is vibrant and bursting with flavors.
- Enjoy the antioxidant-rich goodness of this pomegranate berry delight!

Recipe 92: Turmeric Pineapple Glow Smoothie

Ingredients:
- 1 cup pineapple chunks
- 1/2 teaspoon turmeric powder
- 1 tablespoon honey
- 1 cup coconut water
- Juice of 1/2 lemon
- Ice cubes (optional)

How to Prepare:
- Blend pineapple chunks, turmeric powder, honey, coconut water, and lemon juice until smooth.
- Add ice cubes if desired.
- Blend again until the mixture is glowing with tropical goodness.
- Experience the golden glow of turmeric paired with the sweetness of pineapple!

Recipe 93: Dragon Fruit Berry Bliss Smoothie

Ingredients:
- 1/2 dragon fruit, peeled and chopped
- 1/2 cup raspberries
- 1/2 cup blackberries
- 1 tablespoon honey
- 1 cup coconut water
- Ice cubes (optional)

How to Prepare:
- Blend dragon fruit, raspberries, blackberries, honey, and coconut water until smooth.
- Add ice cubes if desired.
- Blend again until the mixture is visually stunning and deliciously blissful.
- Enjoy the exotic allure of dragon fruit combined with the richness of berries!

Recipe 94: Mango Turmeric Sunrise Smoothie

Ingredients:
- 1 ripe mango, peeled and pitted
- 1/2 teaspoon turmeric powder
- 1/2 teaspoon grated ginger
- 1 tablespoon honey
- 1 cup coconut water
- Ice cubes (optional)

How to Prepare:
- Blend mango, turmeric powder, grated ginger, honey, and coconut water until smooth.
- Add ice cubes if desired.
- Blend again until the mixture is vibrant and energizing like a sunrise.
- Start your day with this mango turmeric delight!

Recipe 95: Acai Berry Powerhouse Smoothie

Ingredients:
- 1 packet frozen acai puree
- 1/2 cup strawberries, hulled
- 1/2 banana
- 1 tablespoon honey
- 1 cup almond milk
- Ice cubes (optional)

How to Prepare:
- Blend acai puree, strawberries, banana, honey, and almond milk until smooth.
- Add ice cubes if desired.
- Blend again until the mixture is rich and packed with antioxidants.
- Experience the power of acai berries in this energizing smoothie!

Recipe 96: Matcha Green Tea Elixir Smoothie

Ingredients:
- 1 teaspoon matcha green tea powder
- 1 banana
- 1 tablespoon honey
- 1 cup almond milk
- 1/2 teaspoon vanilla extract
- Ice cubes (optional)

How to Prepare:
- Blend matcha powder, banana, honey, almond milk, and vanilla extract until smooth.
- Add ice cubes if desired.
- Blend again until the mixture is vibrant and filled with the benefits of matcha.
- Enjoy the antioxidant-rich goodness of this matcha green tea elixir!

Recipe 97: Coconut Mango Spirulina Splash Smoothie

Ingredients:
- 1 ripe mango, peeled and pitted
- 1/2 teaspoon spirulina powder
- 1 tablespoon honey
- 1/2 cup coconut milk
- 1 cup coconut water
- Ice cubes (optional)

How to Prepare:
- Blend mango, spirulina powder, honey, coconut milk, and coconut water until smooth.
- Add ice cubes if desired.
- Blend again until the mixture is tropical and splashing with health benefits.
- Experience the detoxifying power of spirulina with the sweetness of mango and coconut!

Recipe 98: Cacao Peanut Butter Protein Punch Smoothie

Ingredients:
- 2 tablespoons cocoa powder
- 2 tablespoons peanut butter
- 1 scoop chocolate protein powder
- 1 tablespoon honey
- 1 cup almond milk
- Ice cubes (optional)

How to Prepare:
- Blend cocoa powder, peanut butter, chocolate protein powder, honey, and almond milk until smooth.
- Add ice cubes if desired.
- Blend again until the mixture is protein-packed and indulgent.
- Satisfy your chocolate and peanut butter cravings with this protein punch!

Recipe 99: Cherry Almond Chia Delight Smoothie

Ingredients:
- 1 cup cherries, pitted
- 2 tablespoons almond butter
- 1 tablespoon chia seeds
- 1 tablespoon honey
- 1 cup almond milk
- Ice cubes (optional)

How to Prepare:
- Blend cherries, almond butter, chia seeds, honey, and almond milk until smooth.
- Add ice cubes if desired.
- Blend again until the mixture is creamy and delightful.
- Enjoy the satisfying texture of chia seeds in this cherry almond delight!

Recipe 100: Golden Turmeric Coconut Smoothie

Ingredients:
- 1/2 teaspoon turmeric powder
- 1/2 teaspoon cinnamon powder
- 1 tablespoon honey
- 1 cup coconut milk
- 1/2 teaspoon vanilla extract
- Ice cubes (optional)

How to Prepare:
- Blend turmeric powder, cinnamon powder, honey, coconut milk, and vanilla extract until smooth.
- Add ice cubes if desired.
- Blend again until the mixture is golden and filled with warming spices.
- Embrace the comforting flavors of turmeric and cinnamon in this golden smoothie!

ULTIMATE SMOOTHIE SENSATIONS

Recipe 101: Mango Turmeric Lassi Smoothie

Ingredients:
- 1 ripe mango, peeled and pitted
- 1/2 teaspoon turmeric powder
- 1/2 cup plain yogurt
- 1 tablespoon honey
- 1/2 teaspoon cardamom powder
- Ice cubes (optional)

How to Prepare:
- Blend mango, turmeric powder, yogurt, honey, and cardamom powder until smooth.
- Add ice cubes if desired.
- Blend again until the mixture is creamy and has a delightful lassi-like texture.
- Enjoy the Indian-inspired flavors of mango and turmeric!

Recipe 102: Berry Citrus Beet Boost Smoothie

Ingredients:
- 1/2 cup mixed berries (strawberries, blueberries, raspberries)
- 1/2 small beet, peeled and chopped
- Juice of 1 orange
- 1 tablespoon honey
- 1 cup coconut water
- Ice cubes (optional)

How to Prepare:
- Blend mixed berries, beet, orange juice, honey, and coconut water until smooth.
- Add ice cubes if desired.
- Blend again until the mixture is vibrant and packed with antioxidants and vitamins.
- Experience the natural energy boost with this berry citrus beet smoothie!

Recipe 103: Green Goddess Avocado Spinach Smoothie

Ingredients:
- 1/2 ripe avocado, peeled and pitted
- 1 cup spinach leaves
- 1/2 cucumber, peeled and sliced
- 1 tablespoon honey
- Juice of 1/2 lemon
- 1 cup coconut water
- Ice cubes (optional)

How to Prepare:
- Blend avocado, spinach, cucumber, honey, lemon juice, and coconut water until smooth.
- Add ice cubes if desired.
- Blend again until the mixture is refreshing and packed with green goodness.
- Enjoy the creamy texture and health benefits of this green smoothie!

Recipe 104: Peach Basil Breeze Smoothie

Ingredients:
- 2 ripe peaches, peeled and pitted
- 1/4 cup fresh basil leaves
- 1 tablespoon honey
- 1 cup almond milk
- 1/2 teaspoon vanilla extract
- Ice cubes (optional)

How to Prepare:
- Blend peaches, basil leaves, honey, almond milk, and vanilla extract until smooth.
- Add ice cubes if desired.
- Blend again until the mixture is fragrant and bursting with peach-basil flavor.
- Enjoy the unique combination of peaches and basil in this refreshing smoothie!

Recipe 105: Coconut Blue Majik Dream Smoothie

Ingredients:
- 1 cup blueberries
- 1 teaspoon Blue Majik spirulina powder
- 1 tablespoon honey
- 1 cup coconut milk
- 1/2 teaspoon vanilla extract
- Ice cubes (optional)

How to Prepare:
- Blend blueberries, Blue Majik spirulina powder, honey, coconut milk, and vanilla extract until smooth.
- Add ice cubes if desired.
- Blend again until the mixture is vibrant and packed with antioxidants.
- Experience the stunning blue color and health benefits of this unique smoothie!

Recipe 106: **Tropical Carrot Pineapple Punch Smoothie**

Ingredients:
- 1 carrot, peeled and chopped
- 1 cup pineapple chunks
- 1/2 teaspoon grated ginger
- 1 tablespoon honey
- Juice of 1/2 lime
- 1 cup coconut water
- Ice cubes (optional)

How to Prepare:
- Blend carrot, pineapple chunks, ginger, honey, lime juice, and coconut water until smooth.
- Add ice cubes if desired.
- Blend again until the mixture is tropical and revitalizing.
- Enjoy the balance of sweetness from pineapple and the earthy tone from carrots in this punchy smoothie!

Recipe 107: **Raspberry Rosemary Refresher Smoothie**

Ingredients:
- 1 cup raspberries
- 1 teaspoon fresh rosemary leaves
- 1 tablespoon honey
- 1 cup almond milk
- 1/2 teaspoon lemon zest
- Ice cubes (optional)

How to Prepare:
- Blend raspberries, rosemary leaves, honey, almond milk, and lemon zest until smooth.
- Add ice cubes if desired.
- Blend again until the mixture is fragrant and revitalizing.
- Enjoy the aromatic blend of raspberry and rosemary in this refreshing smoothie!

Recipe 108: **Orange Carrot Ginger Zest Smoothie**

Ingredients:
- 2 oranges, peeled and segmented
- 1 carrot, peeled and chopped
- 1/2 teaspoon freshly grated ginger
- 1 tablespoon honey
- 1 cup coconut water

- Ice cubes (optional)

How to Prepare:
- Blend oranges, carrot, ginger, honey, and coconut water until smooth.
- Add ice cubes if desired.
- Blend again until the mixture is zesty and refreshing.
- Experience the invigorating blend of citrus, carrot, and ginger!

Recipe 109: Cacao Raspberry Protein Bliss Smoothie

Ingredients:
- 1 cup raspberries
- 2 tablespoons cocoa powder
- 1 scoop vanilla protein powder
- 1 tablespoon honey
- 1 cup almond milk
- Ice cubes (optional)

How to Prepare:
- Blend raspberries, cocoa powder, vanilla protein powder, honey, and almond milk until smooth.
- Add ice cubes if desired.
- Blend again until the mixture is rich and protein-packed.
- Satisfy your chocolate cravings while boosting your protein intake with this blissful smoothie!

Recipe 110: Chia Cherry Chocolate Delight Smoothie

Ingredients:
- 1 cup cherries, pitted
- 1 tablespoon chia seeds
- 1 tablespoon cocoa powder
- 1 tablespoon honey
- 1 cup almond milk
- Ice cubes (optional)

How to Prepare:
- Blend cherries, chia seeds, cocoa powder, honey, and almond milk until smooth.
- Add ice cubes if desired.
- Blend again until the mixture is thick and delightful.
- Enjoy the delightful texture of chia seeds paired with the classic combination of cherries and chocolate!

Recipe 111: Minty Melon Cooler Smoothie

Ingredients:
- 1 cup honeydew melon, cubed
- 1/2 cup cucumber, peeled and sliced
- 1/4 cup fresh mint leaves
- 1 tablespoon honey
- Juice of 1/2 lime
- 1 cup coconut water
- Ice cubes (optional)

How to Prepare:
- Blend honeydew melon, cucumber, mint leaves, honey, lime juice, and coconut water until smooth.
- Add ice cubes if desired.
- Blend again until the mixture is cool and refreshing.
- Enjoy the hydrating blend of melon and mint!

Recipe 112: Cranberry Apple Cinnamon Smoothie

Ingredients:
- 1/2 cup cranberries, fresh or frozen
- 1 apple, peeled, cored, and chopped
- 1/2 teaspoon ground cinnamon
- 1 tablespoon honey
- 1 cup almond milk
- Ice cubes (optional)

How to Prepare:
- Blend cranberries, apple, cinnamon, honey, and almond milk until smooth.
- Add ice cubes if desired.
- Blend again until the mixture is sweet and spicy.
- Enjoy the autumnal flavors of cranberry, apple, and cinnamon!

Recipe 113: Papaya Coconut Lime Smoothie

Ingredients:
- 1 cup papaya chunks
- 1/2 cup coconut milk
- Juice of 1 lime
- 1 tablespoon honey
- 1 cup coconut water
- Ice cubes (optional)

How to Prepare:
- Blend papaya chunks, coconut milk, lime juice, honey, and coconut water until smooth.
- Add ice cubes if desired.
- Blend again until the mixture is tropical and zesty.
- Experience the exotic blend of papaya, coconut, and lime!

Recipe 114: Fig Pistachio Delight Smoothie

Ingredients:
- 2 ripe figs, stems removed and chopped
- 2 tablespoons shelled pistachios
- 1 tablespoon honey
- 1 cup almond milk
- 1/2 teaspoon vanilla extract
- Ice cubes (optional)

How to Prepare:
- Blend figs, pistachios, honey, almond milk, and vanilla extract until smooth.
- Add ice cubes if desired.
- Blend again until the mixture is creamy and nutty.
- Enjoy the delightful crunch of pistachios in this figgy smoothie!

Recipe 115: Blackberry Lavender Lemonade Smoothie

Ingredients:
- 1 cup blackberries
- 1 teaspoon dried lavender buds (edible)
- Juice of 1/2 lemon
- 1 tablespoon honey
- 1 cup coconut water
- Ice cubes (optional)

How to Prepare:
- Blend blackberries, dried lavender buds, lemon juice, honey, and coconut water until smooth.
- Add ice cubes if desired.
- Blend again until the mixture is fragrant and soothing.
- Experience the calming blend of lavender and the tartness of blackberries!

ULTIMATE SMOOTHIE SENSATIONS

Recipe 116: Apricot Cardamom Cream Smoothie

Ingredients:
- 1 cup apricot halves, pitted
- 1/2 teaspoon ground cardamom
- 1 tablespoon honey
- 1/2 cup Greek yogurt
- 1/2 teaspoon vanilla extract
- Ice cubes (optional)

How to Prepare:
- Blend apricot halves, cardamom, honey, Greek yogurt, and vanilla extract until smooth.
- Add ice cubes if desired.
- Blend again until the mixture is creamy and aromatic.
- Enjoy the exotic blend of apricot and cardamom!

Recipe 117: Cucumber Pineapple Mint Refresher Smoothie

Ingredients:
- 1/2 cucumber, peeled and sliced
- 1 cup pineapple chunks
- 1/4 cup fresh mint leaves
- Juice of 1/2 lime
- 1 tablespoon honey
- 1 cup coconut water
- Ice cubes (optional)

How to Prepare:
- Blend cucumber, pineapple chunks, mint leaves, lime juice, honey, and coconut water until smooth.
- Add ice cubes if desired.
- Blend again until the mixture is cool and revitalizing.
- Enjoy the refreshing blend of cucumber, pineapple, and mint!

Recipe 118: Raspberry Mango Tango Smoothie

Ingredients:
- 1 cup raspberries
- 1 ripe mango, peeled and pitted
- 1 tablespoon honey
- 1/2 teaspoon grated ginger
- 1 cup almond milk
- Ice cubes (optional)

How to Prepare:
- Blend raspberries, mango, honey, grated ginger, and almond milk until smooth.
- Add ice cubes if desired.
- Blend again until the mixture is fruity and invigorating.
- Experience the lively dance of raspberry and mango flavors!

Recipe 119: Matcha Berry Bliss Smoothie

Ingredients:
- 1 teaspoon matcha green tea powder
- 1/2 cup mixed berries (strawberries, blueberries, raspberries)
- 1 tablespoon honey
- 1 cup almond milk
- 1/2 teaspoon vanilla extract
- Ice cubes (optional)

How to Prepare:
- Blend matcha powder, mixed berries, honey, almond milk, and vanilla extract until smooth.
- Add ice cubes if desired.
- Blend again until the mixture is vibrant and filled with the benefits of matcha and antioxidants.
- Enjoy the delightful combination of matcha and mixed berries!

Recipe 120: Chocolate Cherry Almond Indulgence Smoothie

Ingredients:
- 1 cup cherries, pitted
- 2 tablespoons cocoa powder
- 1 tablespoon almond butter
- 1 tablespoon honey
- 1 cup almond milk
- Ice cubes (optional)

How to Prepare:
- Blend cherries, cocoa powder, almond butter, honey, and almond milk until smooth.
- Add ice cubes if desired.
- Blend again until the mixture is rich and indulgent.
- Satisfy your chocolate cravings with this cherry almond delight!

Recipe 121: Spiced Apple Pie Smoothie

Ingredients:
- 1 apple, peeled, cored, and chopped
- 1/2 teaspoon ground cinnamon
- 1/4 teaspoon ground nutmeg
- 1 tablespoon honey
- 1 cup almond milk
- Ice cubes (optional)

How to Prepare:
- Blend chopped apple, cinnamon, nutmeg, honey, and almond milk until smooth.
- Add ice cubes if desired.
- Blend again until the mixture is reminiscent of the classic apple pie flavor.
- Enjoy the taste of autumn in a glass with this spiced apple pie smoothie!

Recipe 122: Coconut Kiwi Kale Kick Smoothie

Ingredients:
- 2 kiwis, peeled and sliced
- 1/2 cup kale leaves, stems removed
- 1/2 cup coconut milk
- 1 tablespoon honey
- Juice of 1/2 lime
- Ice cubes (optional)

How to Prepare:
- Blend kiwis, kale leaves, coconut milk, honey, and lime juice until smooth.
- Add ice cubes if desired.
- Blend again until the mixture is vibrant and packed with nutrients.
- Enjoy the tropical kick of coconut, kiwi, and kale!

Recipe 123: Gingered Pear Smoothie

Ingredients:
- 2 ripe pears, peeled, cored, and chopped
- 1/2 teaspoon freshly grated ginger
- 1 tablespoon honey
- 1 cup almond milk
- 1/2 teaspoon vanilla extract
- Ice cubes (optional)

How to Prepare:
- Blend chopped pears, grated ginger, honey, almond milk, and vanilla extract until smooth.
- Add ice cubes if desired.
- Blend again until the mixture is refreshing and gingery.
- Enjoy the zesty flavor of ginger combined with the sweetness of pears!

Recipe 124: **Mango Basil Bliss Smoothie**

Ingredients:
- 1 ripe mango, peeled and pitted
- 1/4 cup fresh basil leaves
- 1 tablespoon honey
- 1 cup coconut water
- Juice of 1/2 lemon
- Ice cubes (optional)

How to Prepare:
- Blend mango, basil leaves, honey, coconut water, and lemon juice until smooth.
- Add ice cubes if desired.
- Blend again until the mixture is aromatic and revitalizing.
- Experience the delightful fusion of mango and basil!

Recipe 125: **Vanilla Date Delight Smoothie**

Ingredients:
- 3 dates, pitted and chopped
- 1/2 teaspoon vanilla extract
- 1 tablespoon honey
- 1 cup almond milk
- 1 tablespoon almond butter
- Ice cubes (optional)

How to Prepare:
- Blend chopped dates, vanilla extract, honey, almond milk, and almond butter until smooth.
- Add ice cubes if desired.
- Blend again until the mixture is creamy and indulgent.
- Enjoy the natural sweetness of dates in this delightful smoothie!

Recipe 126: Raspberry Coconut Chia Crush Smoothie

Ingredients:
- 1 cup raspberries
- 1/2 cup coconut milk
- 1 tablespoon chia seeds
- 1 tablespoon honey
- 1 cup coconut water
- Ice cubes (optional)

How to Prepare:
- Blend raspberries, coconut milk, chia seeds, honey, and coconut water until smooth.
- Add ice cubes if desired.
- Blend again until the mixture is thick and packed with chia goodness.
- Enjoy the satisfying texture of chia seeds in this raspberry coconut crush!

Recipe 127: Peach Ginger Turmeric Twist Smoothie

Ingredients:
- 2 ripe peaches, peeled and pitted
- 1/2 teaspoon freshly grated ginger
- 1/2 teaspoon turmeric powder
- 1 tablespoon honey
- 1 cup coconut water
- Ice cubes (optional)

How to Prepare:
- Blend peaches, grated ginger, turmeric powder, honey, and coconut water until smooth.
- Add ice cubes if desired.
- Blend again until the mixture is vibrant and refreshing.
- Enjoy the zingy twist of ginger and turmeric with the sweetness of peaches!

Recipe 128: Blueberry Basil Blast Smoothie

Ingredients:
- 1 cup blueberries
- 1/4 cup fresh basil leaves
- 1 tablespoon honey
- 1 cup almond milk
- Juice of 1/2 lemon
- Ice cubes (optional)

How to Prepare:
- Blend blueberries, basil leaves, honey, almond milk, and lemon juice until smooth.
- Add ice cubes if desired.
- Blend again until the mixture is fragrant and bursting with blueberry-basil flavor.
- Experience the refreshing combination of blueberries and basil!

Recipe 129: Cacao Hazelnut Heaven Smoothie

Ingredients:
- 2 tablespoons cocoa powder
- 2 tablespoons hazelnuts
- 1 tablespoon honey
- 1 cup almond milk
- 1/2 teaspoon vanilla extract
- Ice cubes (optional)

How to Prepare:
- Blend cocoa powder, hazelnuts, honey, almond milk, and vanilla extract until smooth.
- Add ice cubes if desired.
- Blend again until the mixture is creamy and heavenly.
- Satisfy your chocolate cravings with this hazelnut delight!

Recipe 130: Mint Chocolate Chip Avocado Smoothie

Ingredients:
- 1/2 ripe avocado, peeled and pitted
- 1 tablespoon cocoa nibs or cocoa powder
- 1/4 cup fresh mint leaves
- 1 tablespoon honey
- 1 cup almond milk
- Ice cubes (optional)

How to Prepare:
- Blend avocado, cocoa nibs, mint leaves, honey, and almond milk until smooth.
- Add ice cubes if desired.
- Blend again until the mixture is creamy and indulgent.
- Enjoy the rich flavors of chocolate and mint with the goodness of avocado!

Recipe 131: Pineapple Turmeric Zinger Smoothie

Ingredients:
- 1 cup pineapple chunks
- 1/2 teaspoon turmeric powder
- 1 tablespoon honey
- 1 cup coconut water
- Juice of 1/2 lemon
- Ice cubes (optional)

How to Prepare:
- Blend pineapple chunks, turmeric powder, honey, coconut water, and lemon juice until smooth.
- Add ice cubes if desired.
- Blend again until the mixture is zesty and refreshing.
- Enjoy the tropical burst of pineapple with the warmth of turmeric!

Recipe 132: Strawberry Basil Serenity Smoothie

Ingredients:
- 1 cup strawberries, hulled
- 1/4 cup fresh basil leaves
- 1 tablespoon honey
- 1 cup almond milk
- 1/2 teaspoon vanilla extract
- Ice cubes (optional)

How to Prepare:
- Blend strawberries, basil leaves, honey, almond milk, and vanilla extract until smooth.
- Add ice cubes if desired.
- Blend again until the mixture is fragrant and calming.
- Experience the harmonious blend of strawberry and basil!

Recipe 133: Coconut Papaya Paradise Smoothie

Ingredients:
- 1 cup papaya chunks
- 1/2 cup coconut milk
- 1 tablespoon honey
- 1 tablespoon shredded coconut (for garnish)
- 1 cup coconut water
- Ice cubes (optional)

How to Prepare:
- Blend papaya chunks, coconut milk, honey, and coconut water until smooth.

- Add ice cubes if desired.
- Blend again until the mixture is tropical and creamy.
- Garnish with shredded coconut before serving for an extra touch of paradise!

Recipe 134: Banana Nutmeg Euphoria Smoothie

Ingredients:
- 2 ripe bananas
- 1/2 teaspoon ground nutmeg
- 1 tablespoon honey
- 1 cup almond milk
- 1 tablespoon almond butter
- Ice cubes (optional)

How to Prepare:
- Blend ripe bananas, nutmeg, honey, almond milk, and almond butter until smooth.
- Add ice cubes if desired.
- Blend again until the mixture is velvety and comforting.
- Enjoy the warm and cozy flavors of banana and nutmeg!

Recipe 135: Raspberry Pineapple Mint Magic Smoothie

Ingredients:
- 1 cup raspberries
- 1 cup pineapple chunks
- 1/4 cup fresh mint leaves
- 1 tablespoon honey
- 1 cup coconut water
- Ice cubes (optional)

How to Prepare:
- Blend raspberries, pineapple chunks, mint leaves, honey, and coconut water until smooth.
- Add ice cubes if desired.
- Blend again until the mixture is vibrant and enchanting.
- Experience the delightful blend of raspberry, pineapple, and mint!

Recipe 136: Cucumber Spinach Kiwi Cleanse Smoothie

Ingredients:
- 1/2 cucumber, peeled and sliced
- 1 cup spinach leaves
- 2 kiwis, peeled and sliced
- 1 tablespoon honey

- Juice of 1/2 lime
- 1 cup coconut water
- Ice cubes (optional)

How to Prepare:
- Blend cucumber, spinach leaves, kiwis, honey, lime juice, and coconut water until smooth.
- Add ice cubes if desired.
- Blend again until the mixture is refreshing and detoxifying.
- Enjoy the cleansing properties of cucumber, spinach, and kiwi!

Recipe 137: Blueberry Lavender Love Smoothie

Ingredients:
- 1 cup blueberries
- 1 teaspoon dried lavender buds (edible)
- 1 tablespoon honey
- 1 cup almond milk
- 1/2 teaspoon vanilla extract
- Ice cubes (optional)

How to Prepare:
- Blend blueberries, dried lavender buds, honey, almond milk, and vanilla extract until smooth.
- Add ice cubes if desired.
- Blend again until the mixture is fragrant and full of love.
- Experience the calming blend of lavender and the sweetness of blueberries!

Recipe 138: Fig Vanilla Dream Smoothie

Ingredients:
- 2 ripe figs, stems removed and chopped
- 1/2 teaspoon vanilla extract
- 1 tablespoon honey
- 1 cup almond milk
- 1 tablespoon chia seeds (for garnish)
- Ice cubes (optional)

How to Prepare:
- Blend figs, vanilla extract, honey, and almond milk until smooth.
- Add ice cubes if desired.
- Blend again until the mixture is creamy and dreamy.
- Garnish with chia seeds before serving for an added crunch!

Recipe 139: Mango Coconut Cardamom Smoothie

Ingredients:
- 1 ripe mango, peeled and pitted
- 1/2 cup coconut milk
- 1/2 teaspoon ground cardamom
- 1 tablespoon honey
- 1 cup coconut water
- Ice cubes (optional)

How to Prepare:
- Blend mango, coconut milk, cardamom, honey, and coconut water until smooth.
- Add ice cubes if desired.
- Blend again until the mixture is exotic and aromatic.
- Enjoy the unique combination of mango, coconut, and cardamom!

Recipe 140: Cherry Vanilla Almond Bliss Smoothie

Ingredients:
- 1 cup cherries, pitted
- 1/2 teaspoon vanilla extract
- 1 tablespoon almond butter
- 1 tablespoon honey
- 1 cup almond milk
- Ice cubes (optional)

How to Prepare:
- Blend cherries, vanilla extract, almond butter, honey, and almond milk until smooth.
- Add ice cubes if desired.
- Blend again until the mixture is creamy and blissful.
- Savor the delightful blend of cherry, vanilla, and almond!

Recipe 141: Melon Mint Medley Smoothie

Ingredients:
- 1 cup mixed melon cubes (watermelon, cantaloupe, honeydew)
- 1/4 cup fresh mint leaves
- 1 tablespoon honey
- Juice of 1/2 lime
- 1 cup coconut water
- Ice cubes (optional)

How to Prepare:
- Blend mixed melon cubes, mint leaves, honey, lime juice, and coconut water until smooth.

- Add ice cubes if desired.
- Blend again until the mixture is refreshing and delightful.
- Enjoy the cool, minty freshness of this melon medley smoothie!

Recipe 142: Cinnamon Pear Pleasure Smoothie

Ingredients:
- 2 ripe pears, peeled, cored, and chopped
- 1/2 teaspoon ground cinnamon
- 1 tablespoon honey
- 1 cup almond milk
- 1/2 teaspoon vanilla extract
- Ice cubes (optional)

How to Prepare:
- Blend chopped pears, cinnamon, honey, almond milk, and vanilla extract until smooth.
- Add ice cubes if desired.
- Blend again until the mixture is cozy and comforting.
- Enjoy the warm, spiced flavors of cinnamon and pear!

Recipe 143: Kiwi Lime Kale Kick Smoothie

Ingredients:
- 2 kiwis, peeled and sliced
- Juice of 1 lime
- 1/2 cup kale leaves, stems removed
- 1 tablespoon honey
- 1 cup coconut water
- Ice cubes (optional)

How to Prepare:
- Blend kiwis, lime juice, kale leaves, honey, and coconut water until smooth.
- Add ice cubes if desired.
- Blend again until the mixture is vibrant and invigorating.
- Experience the tangy kick of kiwi and lime combined with the goodness of kale!

Recipe 144: Banana Berry Basil Bliss Smoothie

Ingredients:
- 1 ripe banana
- 1/2 cup mixed berries (strawberries, blueberries, raspberries)
- 1/4 cup fresh basil leaves
- 1 tablespoon honey

- 1 cup almond milk
- Ice cubes (optional)

How to Prepare:
- Blend ripe banana, mixed berries, basil leaves, honey, and almond milk until smooth.
- Add ice cubes if desired.
- Blend again until the mixture is fragrant and blissful.
- Enjoy the delightful blend of banana, berries, and basil!

Recipe 145: Raspberry Rose Refresher Smoothie

Ingredients:
- 1 cup raspberries
- 1 teaspoon rose water (food grade)
- 1 tablespoon honey
- 1 cup almond milk
- 1/2 teaspoon vanilla extract
- Ice cubes (optional)

How to Prepare:
- Blend raspberries, rose water, honey, almond milk, and vanilla extract until smooth.
- Add ice cubes if desired.
- Blend again until the mixture is fragrant and reminiscent of a rose garden.
- Experience the delicate aroma and taste of rose in this refreshing smoothie!

Recipe 146: Minty Chocolate Chip Delight Smoothie

Ingredients:
- 1/2 ripe avocado, peeled and pitted
- 1 tablespoon cocoa nibs or mini chocolate chips
- 1/4 cup fresh mint leaves
- 1 tablespoon honey
- 1 cup almond milk
- Ice cubes (optional)

How to Prepare:
- Blend avocado, cocoa nibs, mint leaves, honey, and almond milk until smooth.
- Add ice cubes if desired.
- Blend again until the mixture is creamy and indulgent.
- Enjoy the classic combination of mint and chocolate in a healthier form!

Recipe 147: Chia Berry Citrus Splash Smoothie

Ingredients:
- 1/2 cup mixed berries (strawberries, blueberries, raspberries)
- 1 tablespoon chia seeds
- Juice of 1/2 orange
- Juice of 1/2 lemon
- 1 tablespoon honey
- 1 cup coconut water
- Ice cubes (optional)

How to Prepare:
- Blend mixed berries, chia seeds, orange juice, lemon juice, honey, and coconut water until smooth.
- Add ice cubes if desired.
- Blend again until the mixture is vibrant and bursting with citrus flavor.
- Enjoy the delightful crunch of chia seeds and the refreshing citrusy splash!

Recipe 148: Peach Raspberry Rosemary Smoothie

Ingredients:
- 2 ripe peaches, peeled and pitted
- 1 cup raspberries
- 1 teaspoon fresh rosemary leaves
- 1 tablespoon honey
- 1 cup almond milk
- Ice cubes (optional)

How to Prepare:
- Blend peaches, raspberries, rosemary leaves, honey, and almond milk until smooth.
- Add ice cubes if desired.
- Blend again until the mixture is aromatic and bursting with fruity goodness.
- Experience the unique blend of peach, raspberry, and rosemary!

Recipe 149: Orange Carrot Turmeric Twist Smoothie

Ingredients:
- 2 oranges, peeled and segmented
- 1 carrot, peeled and chopped
- 1/2 teaspoon turmeric powder
- 1 tablespoon honey
- 1 cup coconut water

- Ice cubes (optional)

How to Prepare:
- Blend oranges, carrot, turmeric powder, honey, and coconut water until smooth.
- Add ice cubes if desired.
- Blend again until the mixture is vibrant and packed with vitamins.
- Enjoy the zesty twist of orange combined with the earthy goodness of carrot and turmeric!

Recipe 150: Mango Pineapple Basil Bliss Smoothie

Ingredients:
- 1 ripe mango, peeled and pitted
- 1 cup pineapple chunks
- 1/4 cup fresh basil leaves
- 1 tablespoon honey
- 1 cup coconut water
- Ice cubes (optional)

How to Prepare:
- Blend mango, pineapple chunks, basil leaves, honey, and coconut water until smooth.
- Add ice cubes if desired.
- Blend again until the mixture is aromatic and tropical.
- Enjoy the heavenly combination of mango, pineapple, and basil!

Recipe 151: Cocoa Banana Peanut Butter Crunch Smoothie

Ingredients:
- 2 ripe bananas
- 2 tablespoons cocoa powder
- 2 tablespoons peanut butter
- 1 tablespoon honey
- 1 cup almond milk
- Ice cubes (optional)

How to Prepare:
- Blend ripe bananas, cocoa powder, peanut butter, honey, and almond milk until smooth.
- Add ice cubes if desired.
- Blend again until the mixture is creamy and indulgent.
- Enjoy the rich chocolatey flavor with a satisfying crunch from peanut butter!

Recipe 152: **Blackberry Sage Sensation Smoothie**

Ingredients:
- 1 cup blackberries
- 1 tablespoon fresh sage leaves
- 1 tablespoon honey
- 1 cup almond milk
- Juice of 1/2 lemon
- Ice cubes (optional)

How to Prepare:
- Blend blackberries, sage leaves, honey, almond milk, and lemon juice until smooth.
- Add ice cubes if desired.
- Blend again until the mixture is fragrant and delightful.
- Experience the unique combination of blackberry and sage!

Recipe 153: **Pineapple Coconut Matcha Madness Smoothie**

Ingredients:
- 1 cup pineapple chunks
- 1/2 cup coconut milk
- 1 teaspoon matcha green tea powder
- 1 tablespoon honey
- 1 cup coconut water
- Ice cubes (optional)

How to Prepare:
- Blend pineapple chunks, coconut milk, matcha powder, honey, and coconut water until smooth.
- Add ice cubes if desired.
- Blend again until the mixture is vibrant and energizing.
- Enjoy the antioxidant-packed matcha with the tropical flavors of pineapple and coconut!

Recipe 154: **Fig Date Walnut Wonder Smoothie**

Ingredients:
- 2 ripe figs, stems removed and chopped
- 3 dates, pitted and chopped
- 2 tablespoons walnuts
- 1 tablespoon honey
- 1 cup almond milk
- Ice cubes (optional)

How to Prepare:
- Blend figs, dates, walnuts, honey, and almond milk until smooth.
- Add ice cubes if desired.
- Blend again until the mixture is rich and satisfying.
- Savor the natural sweetness of figs and dates with the crunch of walnuts!

Recipe 155: Mango Spinach Ginger Glow Smoothie

Ingredients:
- 1 ripe mango, peeled and pitted
- 1 cup spinach leaves
- 1/2 teaspoon freshly grated ginger
- 1 tablespoon honey
- Juice of 1/2 lime
- 1 cup coconut water
- Ice cubes (optional)

How to Prepare:
- Blend mango, spinach leaves, ginger, honey, lime juice, and coconut water until smooth.
- Add ice cubes if desired.
- Blend again until the mixture is vibrant and refreshing.
- Experience the glow of health with this mango-spinach delight!

Recipe 156: Blueberry Basil Blast Smoothie

Ingredients:
- 1 cup blueberries
- 1/4 cup fresh basil leaves
- 1 tablespoon honey
- 1 cup almond milk
- Juice of 1/2 lemon
- Ice cubes (optional)

How to Prepare:
- Blend blueberries, basil leaves, honey, almond milk, and lemon juice until smooth.
- Add ice cubes if desired.
- Blend again until the mixture is fragrant and bursting with blueberry-basil flavor.
- Experience the refreshing combination of blueberries and basil!

Recipe 157: Cherry Almond Spice Smoothie

Ingredients:
- 1 cup cherries, pitted
- 2 tablespoons almond butter
- 1/2 teaspoon ground cinnamon
- 1 tablespoon honey
- 1 cup almond milk
- Ice cubes (optional)

How to Prepare:
- Blend cherries, almond butter, cinnamon, honey, and almond milk until smooth.
- Add ice cubes if desired.
- Blend again until the mixture is creamy and spiced.
- Enjoy the warm, comforting flavors of cherry, almond, and cinnamon!

Recipe 158: Papaya Pineapple Basil Bliss Smoothie

Ingredients:
- 1 cup papaya chunks
- 1 cup pineapple chunks
- 1/4 cup fresh basil leaves
- 1 tablespoon honey
- 1 cup coconut water
- Ice cubes (optional)

How to Prepare:
- Blend papaya chunks, pineapple chunks, basil leaves, honey, and coconut water until smooth.
- Add ice cubes if desired.
- Blend again until the mixture is aromatic and tropical.
- Experience the heavenly blend of papaya, pineapple, and basil!

Recipe 159: Strawberry Mango Maca Marvel Smoothie

Ingredients:
- 1 cup strawberries, hulled
- 1 ripe mango, peeled and pitted
- 1 teaspoon maca powder
- 1 tablespoon honey
- 1 cup almond milk
- Ice cubes (optional)

How to Prepare:
- Blend strawberries, mango, maca powder, honey, and almond milk

until smooth.
- Add ice cubes if desired.
- Blend again until the mixture is vibrant and energizing.
- Enjoy the nutrient-packed goodness of maca with the sweetness of strawberries and mango!

Recipe 160: Coconut Cherry Chia Delight Smoothie

Ingredients:
- 1 cup cherries, pitted
- 1/2 cup coconut milk
- 1 tablespoon chia seeds
- 1 tablespoon honey
- 1 cup coconut water
- Ice cubes (optional)

How to Prepare:
- Blend cherries, coconut milk, chia seeds, honey, and coconut water until smooth.
- Add ice cubes if desired.
- Blend again until the mixture is thick and chia-infused.
- Enjoy the satisfying texture of chia seeds in this coconut-cherry delight!

Recipe 161: Pomegranate Blueberry Basil Boost Smoothie

Ingredients:
- 1/2 cup pomegranate seeds
- 1 cup blueberries
- 1/4 cup fresh basil leaves
- 1 tablespoon honey
- 1 cup almond milk
- Ice cubes (optional)

How to Prepare:
- Blend pomegranate seeds, blueberries, basil leaves, honey, and almond milk until smooth.
- Add ice cubes if desired.
- Blend again until the mixture is antioxidant-rich and refreshing.
- Enjoy the burst of flavors from this vibrant smoothie!

Recipe 162: Cucumber Mint Green Goodness Smoothie

Ingredients:
- 1/2 cucumber, peeled and sliced
- 1/4 cup fresh mint leaves

- 1 cup spinach leaves
- 1 tablespoon honey
- Juice of 1/2 lime
- 1 cup coconut water
- Ice cubes (optional)

How to Prepare:
- Blend cucumber, mint leaves, spinach leaves, honey, lime juice, and coconut water until smooth.
- Add ice cubes if desired.
- Blend again until the mixture is green, refreshing, and packed with nutrients.
- Enjoy the clean and crisp taste of this green goodness smoothie!

Recipe 163: Raspberry Mango Macadamia Magic Smoothie

Ingredients:
- 1 cup raspberries
- 1 ripe mango, peeled and pitted
- 2 tablespoons macadamia nuts
- 1 tablespoon honey
- 1 cup almond milk
- Ice cubes (optional)

How to Prepare:
- Blend raspberries, mango, macadamia nuts, honey, and almond milk until smooth.
- Add ice cubes if desired.
- Blend again until the mixture is creamy and indulgent.
- Experience the tropical paradise in a glass with this smoothie!

Recipe 164: Carrot Pineapple Turmeric Twist Smoothie

Ingredients:
- 1 carrot, peeled and chopped
- 1 cup pineapple chunks
- 1/2 teaspoon turmeric powder
- 1 tablespoon honey
- 1 cup coconut water
- Ice cubes (optional)

How to Prepare:
- Blend carrot, pineapple chunks, turmeric powder, honey, and coconut water until smooth.
- Add ice cubes if desired.
- Blend again until the mixture is vibrant and immune-boosting.
- Enjoy the tropical twist with the benefits of turmeric!

Recipe 165: Avocado Kale Citrus Splash Smoothie

Ingredients:
- 1/2 ripe avocado, peeled and pitted
- 1/2 cup kale leaves, stems removed
- Juice of 1 orange
- Juice of 1/2 lemon
- 1 tablespoon honey
- 1 cup coconut water

Ice cubes (optional)

How to Prepare:
- Blend avocado, kale leaves, orange juice, lemon juice, honey, and coconut water until smooth.
- Add ice cubes if desired.
- Blend again until the mixture is creamy and citrusy.
- Enjoy the creamy texture with a refreshing citrus splash!

Recipe 166: Spinach Mango Ginger Zing Smoothie

Ingredients:
- 1 cup spinach leaves
- 1 ripe mango, peeled and pitted
- 1/2 teaspoon freshly grated ginger
- 1 tablespoon honey
- 1 cup almond milk
- Ice cubes (optional)

How to Prepare:
- Blend spinach leaves, mango, ginger, honey, and almond milk until smooth.
- Add ice cubes if desired.
- Blend again until the mixture is vibrant and zesty.
- Experience the energizing zing of ginger in this nutritious smoothie!

Recipe 167: Strawberry Pineapple Basil Bliss Smoothie

Ingredients:
- 1 cup strawberries, hulled
- 1 cup pineapple chunks
- 1/4 cup fresh basil leaves
- 1 tablespoon honey
- 1 cup coconut water
- Ice cubes (optional)

How to Prepare:
- Blend strawberries, pineapple chunks, basil leaves, honey, and coconut water until smooth.
- Add ice cubes if desired.
- Blend again until the mixture is aromatic and tropical.
- Enjoy the heavenly combination of strawberry, pineapple, and basil!

Recipe 168: Cocoa Coconut Almond Indulgence Smoothie

Ingredients:
- 2 tablespoons cocoa powder
- 1/2 cup coconut milk
- 2 tablespoons almond butter
- 1 tablespoon honey
- 1 cup almond milk
- Ice cubes (optional)

How to Prepare:
- Blend cocoa powder, coconut milk, almond butter, honey, and almond milk until smooth.
- Add ice cubes if desired.
- Blend again until the mixture is creamy and indulgent.
- Satisfy your chocolate cravings guilt-free with this delightful smoothie!

Recipe 169: Peach Raspberry Rosemary Refresh Smoothie

Ingredients:
- 2 ripe peaches, peeled and pitted
- 1 cup raspberries
- 1 teaspoon fresh rosemary leaves
- 1 tablespoon honey
- 1 cup almond milk
- Ice cubes (optional)

How to Prepare:
- Blend peaches, raspberries, rosemary leaves, honey, and almond milk until smooth.
- Add ice cubes if desired.
- Blend again until the mixture is aromatic and bursting with fruity goodness.
- Experience the unique blend of peach, raspberry, and rosemary!

Recipe 170: Mango Pineapple Basil Bliss Smoothie

Ingredients:
- 1 ripe mango, peeled and pitted
- 1 cup pineapple chunks
- 1/4 cup fresh basil leaves
- 1 tablespoon honey
- 1 cup coconut water
- Ice cubes (optional)

How to Prepare:
- Blend mango, pineapple chunks, basil leaves, honey, and coconut water until smooth.
- Add ice cubes if desired.
- Blend again until the mixture is aromatic and tropical.
- Enjoy the heavenly combination of mango, pineapple, and basil!

Recipe 171: Raspberry Lemonade Twist Smoothie

Ingredients:
- 1 cup raspberries
- Juice of 2 lemons
- 1 tablespoon honey
- 1 cup coconut water
- Ice cubes (optional)
- Fresh mint leaves for garnish (optional)

How to Prepare:
- Blend raspberries, lemon juice, honey, and coconut water until smooth.
- Add ice cubes if desired and blend again.
- Garnish with fresh mint leaves for a refreshing twist.
- Enjoy the tangy goodness of raspberry lemonade in a smoothie form!

Recipe 172: Banana Chia Seed Power Smoothie

Ingredients:
- 2 ripe bananas
- 2 tablespoons chia seeds
- 1 tablespoon honey
- 1 cup almond milk
- 1/2 teaspoon vanilla extract
- Ice cubes (optional)

How to Prepare:
- Blend ripe bananas, chia seeds, honey, almond milk, and vanilla

ULTIMATE SMOOTHIE SENSATIONS

- extract until smooth.
- Add ice cubes if desired and blend again.
- Experience the energy-boosting power of chia seeds combined with the creaminess of bananas.

Recipe 173: Blueberry Lavender Lemonade Smoothie

Ingredients:
- 1 cup blueberries
- 1 teaspoon dried lavender buds (edible)
- Juice of 1 lemon
- 1 tablespoon honey
- 1 cup almond milk
- Ice cubes (optional)

How to Prepare:
- Blend blueberries, dried lavender buds, lemon juice, honey, and almond milk until smooth.
- Add ice cubes if desired and blend again.
- Enjoy the calming aroma of lavender combined with the zesty freshness of lemon.

Recipe 174: Orange Mango Carrot Sunshine Smoothie

Ingredients:
- 2 oranges, peeled and segmented
- 1 ripe mango, peeled and pitted
- 1 carrot, peeled and chopped
- 1 tablespoon honey
- 1 cup coconut water
- Ice cubes (optional)

How to Prepare:
- Blend oranges, mango, carrot, honey, and coconut water until smooth.
- Add ice cubes if desired and blend again.
- Experience the sunny blend of orange, mango, and carrot that brightens up your day.

Recipe 175: Cocoa Banana Berry Bliss Smoothie

Ingredients:
- 1 ripe banana
- 1 cup mixed berries (strawberries, blueberries, raspberries)
- 2 tablespoons cocoa powder
- 1 tablespoon honey

- 1 cup almond milk
- Ice cubes (optional)

How to Prepare:
- Blend ripe banana, mixed berries, cocoa powder, honey, and almond milk until smooth.
- Add ice cubes if desired and blend again.
- Indulge in the rich chocolaty goodness with the sweetness of berries and banana.

Recipe 176: Pineapple Kale Coconut Cooler Smoothie

Ingredients:
- 1 cup pineapple chunks
- 1/2 cup kale leaves, stems removed
- 1/2 cup coconut milk
- 1 tablespoon honey
- 1 cup coconut water
- Ice cubes (optional)

How to Prepare:
- Blend pineapple chunks, kale leaves, coconut milk, honey, and coconut water until smooth.
- Add ice cubes if desired and blend again.
- Enjoy the tropical freshness with the added nutrition of kale.

Recipe 177: Mango Turmeric Ginger Gold Smoothie

Ingredients:
- 1 ripe mango, peeled and pitted
- 1/2 teaspoon ground turmeric
- 1/2 teaspoon freshly grated ginger
- 1 tablespoon honey
- 1 cup almond milk
- Ice cubes (optional)

How to Prepare:
- Blend mango, turmeric, ginger, honey, and almond milk until smooth.
- Add ice cubes if desired and blend again.
- Embrace the golden blend of mango, turmeric, and ginger for a healthy kick.

Recipe 178: Berry Spinach Flax Fuel Smoothie

Ingredients:
- 1 cup mixed berries (strawberries, blueberries, raspberries)
- 1 cup spinach leaves
- 1 tablespoon ground flaxseeds
- 1 tablespoon honey
- 1 cup almond milk
- Ice cubes (optional)

How to Prepare:
- Blend mixed berries, spinach leaves, flaxseeds, honey, and almond milk until smooth.
- Add ice cubes if desired and blend again.
- Fuel your day with the power of berries, spinach, and flaxseeds.

Recipe 179: Coconut Kiwi Lime Paradise Smoothie

Ingredients:
- 2 kiwis, peeled and sliced
- Juice of 2 limes
- 1/2 cup coconut milk
- 1 tablespoon honey
- 1 cup coconut water
- Ice cubes (optional)

How to Prepare:
- Blend kiwis, lime juice, coconut milk, honey, and coconut water until smooth.
- Add ice cubes if desired and blend again.
- Transport yourself to paradise with the tropical blend of kiwi, lime, and coconut.

Recipe 180: Cherry Vanilla Protein Punch Smoothie

Ingredients:
- 1 cup cherries, pitted
- 1 scoop vanilla protein powder
- 1 tablespoon almond butter
- 1 tablespoon honey
- 1 cup almond milk
- Ice cubes (optional)

How to Prepare:
- Blend cherries, vanilla protein powder, almond butter, honey, and almond milk until smooth.
- Add ice cubes if desired and blend again.

- Power up your day with this protein-packed cherry vanilla delight.

Recipe 181: Raspberry **Mango** Basil Bliss Smoothie

Ingredients:
- 1 cup raspberries
- 1 ripe mango, peeled and pitted
- 1/4 cup fresh basil leaves
- 1 tablespoon honey
- 1 cup coconut water
- Ice cubes (optional)

How to Prepare:
- Blend raspberries, mango, basil leaves, honey, and coconut water until smooth.
- Add ice cubes if desired and blend again.
- Experience the delightful fusion of raspberry, mango, and basil.

Recipe 182: Papaya **Pineapple** Mint Medley Smoothie

Ingredients:
- 1 cup papaya chunks
- 1 cup pineapple chunks
- 1/4 cup fresh mint leaves
- 1 tablespoon honey
- 1 cup coconut water
- Ice cubes (optional)

How to Prepare:
- Blend papaya chunks, pineapple chunks, mint leaves, honey, and coconut water until smooth.
- Add ice cubes if desired and blend again.
- Enjoy the tropical medley of papaya, pineapple, and mint.

Recipe 183: Blueberry **Almond** Butter Crunch Smoothie

Ingredients:
- 1 cup blueberries
- 2 tablespoons almond butter
- 1 tablespoon honey
- 1 cup almond milk
- 1/4 cup granola
- Ice cubes (optional)

How to Prepare:
- Blend blueberries, almond butter, honey, and almond milk until

smooth.
- Add ice cubes if desired and blend again.
- Pour into a glass, top with granola for a delightful crunch.
- Savor the creamy blend with a nutty crunch.

Recipe 184: Chia Coconut Berry Burst Smoothie

Ingredients:
- 1/2 cup mixed berries (strawberries, blueberries, raspberries)
- 1 tablespoon chia seeds
- 1/2 cup coconut milk
- 1 tablespoon honey
- 1 cup coconut water
- Ice cubes (optional)

How to Prepare:
- Blend mixed berries, chia seeds, coconut milk, honey, and coconut water until smooth.
- Add ice cubes if desired and blend again.
- Revel in the burst of flavors with the added texture from chia seeds.

Recipe 185: Mango Turmeric Citrus Zing Smoothie

Ingredients:
- 1 ripe mango, peeled and pitted
- 1/2 teaspoon ground turmeric
- Juice of 1 orange
- Juice of 1/2 lemon
- 1 tablespoon honey
- 1 cup coconut water
- Ice cubes (optional)

How to Prepare:
- Blend mango, turmeric, orange juice, lemon juice, honey, and coconut water until smooth.
- Add ice cubes if desired and blend again.
- Enjoy the zesty and anti-inflammatory blend.

Recipe 186: Peach Raspberry Rosewater Elegance Smoothie

Ingredients:
- 2 ripe peaches, peeled and pitted
- 1 cup raspberries
- 1 teaspoon rosewater (food grade)
- 1 tablespoon honey

- 1 cup almond milk
- Ice cubes (optional)

How to Prepare:
- Blend peaches, raspberries, rosewater, honey, and almond milk until smooth.
- Add ice cubes if desired and blend again.
- Experience the elegant aroma and taste of rose in this refreshing smoothie.

Recipe 187: Cocoa Banana Coconut Crunch Smoothie

Ingredients:
- 2 ripe bananas
- 2 tablespoons cocoa powder
- 1/2 cup coconut milk
- 1 tablespoon honey
- 1/4 cup shredded coconut
- Ice cubes (optional)

How to Prepare:
- Blend ripe bananas, cocoa powder, coconut milk, honey, and half of the shredded coconut until smooth.
- Add ice cubes if desired and blend again.
- Pour into a glass, sprinkle the remaining shredded coconut on top.
- Indulge in the creamy chocolaty delight with a coconut crunch.

Recipe 188: Kiwi Spinach Green Goddess Smoothie

Ingredients:
- 2 kiwis, peeled and sliced
- 1 cup spinach leaves
- 1/2 cup coconut water
- 1 tablespoon honey
- Juice of 1/2 lime
- Ice cubes (optional)

How to Prepare:
- Blend kiwis, spinach leaves, coconut water, honey, and lime juice until smooth.
- Add ice cubes if desired and blend again.
- Embrace the green goodness with the tropical touch of kiwi.

ULTIMATE SMOOTHIE SENSATIONS

Recipe 189: Strawberry Pine Nut Dream Smoothie

Ingredients:
- 1 cup strawberries, hulled
- 2 tablespoons pine nuts
- 1 tablespoon honey
- 1 cup almond milk
- 1/2 teaspoon vanilla extract
- Ice cubes (optional)

How to Prepare:
- Blend strawberries, pine nuts, honey, almond milk, and vanilla extract until smooth.
- Add ice cubes if desired and blend again.
- Enjoy the unique blend of strawberry sweetness and pine nut richness.

Recipe 190: Orange Carrot Ginger Energizer Smoothie

Ingredients:
- 2 oranges, peeled and segmented
- 1 carrot, peeled and chopped
- 1/2 teaspoon freshly grated ginger
- 1 tablespoon honey
- 1 cup coconut water
- Ice cubes (optional)

How to Prepare:
- Blend oranges, carrot, ginger, honey, and coconut water until smooth.
- Add ice cubes if desired and blend again.
- Feel energized with the zesty orange and the warmth of ginger.

Recipe 191: Minty Melon Cucumber Cooler Smoothie

Ingredients:
- 1 cup honeydew melon chunks
- 1/2 cucumber, peeled and sliced
- 1/4 cup fresh mint leaves
- 1 tablespoon honey
- 1 cup coconut water; Ice cubes (optional)

How to Prepare:
- Blend honeydew melon chunks, cucumber, mint leaves, honey, and coconut water until smooth. Add ice cubes if desired; blend again.
- Enjoy the refreshing coolness of melon and cucumber with a hint of mint.

ULTIMATE SMOOTHIE SENSATIONS

Recipe 192: Cinnamon Apple Oatmeal Smoothie

Ingredients:
- 1 apple, peeled, cored, and chopped
- 2 tablespoons rolled oats
- 1/2 teaspoon ground cinnamon
- 1 tablespoon honey
- 1 cup almond milk
- Ice cubes (optional)

How to Prepare:
- Blend apple, rolled oats, cinnamon, honey, and almond milk until smooth.
- Add ice cubes if desired and blend again.
- Experience the comforting flavors of apple pie in a healthy smoothie form.

Recipe 193: Cherry Coconut Lime Delight Smoothie

Ingredients:
- 1 cup cherries, pitted
- 1/2 cup coconut milk
- Juice of 1 lime
- 1 tablespoon honey
- 1 cup coconut water
- Ice cubes (optional)

How to Prepare:
- Blend cherries, coconut milk, lime juice, honey, and coconut water until smooth.
- Add ice cubes if desired and blend again.
- Revel in the tropical fusion of cherry, coconut, and lime.

Recipe 194: Peach Raspberry Pecan Pleasure Smoothie

Ingredients:
- 2 ripe peaches, peeled and pitted
- 1 cup raspberries
- 2 tablespoons pecans
- 1 tablespoon honey
- 1 cup almond milk
- Ice cubes (optional)

How to Prepare:
- Blend peaches, raspberries, pecans, honey, and almond milk until smooth.
- Add ice cubes if desired and blend again.

ULTIMATE SMOOTHIE SENSATIONS

- Enjoy the delightful combination of peach sweetness and raspberry tartness, with a crunch of pecans.

Recipe 195: Avocado Blueberry Basil Beauty Smoothie

Ingredients:
- 1/2 ripe avocado, peeled and pitted
- 1 cup blueberries
- 1/4 cup fresh basil leaves
- 1 tablespoon honey
- 1 cup coconut water
- Ice cubes (optional)

How to Prepare:
- Blend avocado, blueberries, basil leaves, honey, and coconut water until smooth.
- Add ice cubes if desired and blend again.
- Experience the creamy texture with the burst of blueberry and basil freshness.

Recipe 196: Mango Pine Nut Paradise Smoothie

Ingredients:
- 1 ripe mango, peeled and pitted
- 2 tablespoons pine nuts
- 1 tablespoon honey
- 1 cup almond milk
- 1/2 teaspoon vanilla extract
- Ice cubes (optional)

How to Prepare:
- Blend mango, pine nuts, honey, almond milk, and vanilla extract until smooth.
- Add ice cubes if desired and blend again.
- Enjoy the tropical sweetness of mango combined with the richness of pine nuts.

Recipe 197: Strawberry Almond Poppy Seed Smoothie

Ingredients:
- 1 cup strawberries, hulled
- 2 tablespoons almond butter
- 1 teaspoon poppy seeds
- 1 tablespoon honey
- 1 cup almond milk
- Ice cubes (optional)

How to Prepare:
- Blend strawberries, almond butter, poppy seeds, honey, and almond milk until smooth.
- Add ice cubes if desired and blend again.
- Delight in the nutty essence of almond butter and the crunch of poppy seeds.

Recipe 198: Pineapple Chia Coconut Bliss Smoothie

Ingredients:
- 1 cup pineapple chunks
- 1 tablespoon chia seeds
- 1/2 cup coconut milk
- 1 tablespoon honey
- 1 cup coconut water
- Ice cubes (optional)

How to Prepare:
- Blend pineapple chunks, chia seeds, coconut milk, honey, and coconut water until smooth.
- Add ice cubes if desired and blend again.
- Experience the tropical blend with the added texture of chia seeds.

Recipe 199: Cocoa Raspberry Hazelnut Heaven Smoothie

Ingredients:
- 1 cup raspberries
- 2 tablespoons cocoa powder
- 2 tablespoons crushed hazelnuts
- 1 tablespoon honey
- 1 cup almond milk
- Ice cubes (optional)

How to Prepare:
- Blend raspberries, cocoa powder, crushed hazelnuts, honey, and almond milk until smooth.
- Add ice cubes if desired and blend again.
- Indulge in the chocolatey richness with the crunch of hazelnuts.

Recipe 200: Orange Carrot Turmeric Radiance Smoothie

Ingredients:
- 2 oranges, peeled and segmented
- 1 carrot, peeled and chopped
- 1/2 teaspoon ground turmeric
- 1 tablespoon honey
- 1 cup coconut water
- Ice cubes (optional)

How to Prepare:
- Blend oranges, carrot, turmeric, honey, and coconut water until smooth.
- Add ice cubes if desired and blend again.
- Glow with the radiance of this vitamin-packed, anti-inflammatory smoothie.

Conclusion: Sip Your Way to Vibrant Living

As you turn the last page of Ultimate Smoothie Sensations, you'll realize that you've started on a life-changing adventure through the realms of taste, health, and nutrition. You've discovered new blending techniques with each recipe, making delicious and healthy drinks that satisfy your cravings. You may now create wonderful experiences from the most mundane items thanks to your blender's magical abilities.

This book, however, is not only a compilation of dishes. It's a manual to help you live longer, stronger, and healthier. You now have the skills to take a regular smoothie to the next level, thanks to the knowledge you gained here about flavor blending, the importance of using healthy components, and more.

Your health and wellbeing are in your own hands. The ingredients in each smoothie are not only beneficial to your physical health but also to your mental acuity, vitality, and disposition. What you put into your body, mind, and spirit is equally as important as what you put into it on this trip.

Every glass you drink brings you closer to a healthy you. Whether your goal is to shed pounds, gain energy, or simply satisfy your taste buds, you'll find a smoothie here that fits the bill. They're more than simply a drink; they're a toast to your health and vigor.

Don't be afraid to try new things when you go out into the world and use what you've learned. Change things up and come up with your own unique combinations. If you just let your imagination go wild, you'll find that eating well can be just as much fun as it is good for you.

Holding Ultimate Smoothie Sensations in your hands is more than simply a way of life. A way of life where each component is deliberate, each combination is a step toward health, and each sip is a reminder that you are putting money toward your greatest asset: your wellbeing.

So, cheers to you, the fitness fanatic, the foodie, and the traveler who knows that health is an ongoing process, not a final destination. I hope the road you take toward a more vivacious lifestyle is as enjoyable as the smoothies you whip up in the blender.

Cheers to your vibrant, healthy life! Happy blending!

Printed in Great Britain
by Amazon